The Complete Films of
EISENSTEIN

together with an unpublished essay by
Eisenstein ,S

translated by John Hetherington

Weidenfeld and Nicolson
London

Selected from the Avant-Scène Cinéma archives with the
collaboration of the S.M.Eisenstein Memorial Centre (Moscow), 250
stills from Eisenstein's ten films appear in this original work, and an
essay by Eisenstein never before published in England is included as a
foreword.

The plates contained in this book are frame enlargements, apart from
seven particularly interesting publicity stills. The authenticity of the
plates is considered to be more important than the sharpness of certain
'action' pictures, which have been left unretouched intentionally.

This work was produced under the direction of Jacques Charrière
and designed by Jacques Maillot, with a commentary by Abraham
Segal.

First published in French by Société Nouvelle des Editions du Chêne
© Société Nouvelle des Editions du Chêne
This translation © Weidenfeld and Nicolson 11 St John's Hill
London SW11
ISBN 0 297 76725 9

Filmset by Keyspools Ltd, Golborne, Lancashire
Printed in France by Héliogravure Humblot,
Nancy Dépôt légal n° 5260/3/1974

Contents

The Close-up (unpublished essay by Eisenstein)   4

Filmography, Biography and Bibliography   10

Gloumov's Diary   15

Strike   19

The Battleship *Potemkin*   31

October   51

The General Line   69

Que Viva Mexico   79

Bezhin Meadow   89

Alexander Nevsky   99

The Fergana Canal   125

Ivan the Terrible   127

S.M. EISENSTEIN

The Close-up

A branch of lilac.
White,
double.

In the lush green of the leaves.

Bathed in the blinding rays of the sun.

It bursts in through the window.

It sways above the window-sill.
And becomes the first childhood
impression I can recollect.

A close-up!

A close-up of a white lilac swaying over
my cradle is my first childhood
impression.

However, it is no cradle. It is a little
white bed with nickel-plated little balls
on the four posts and a white net
between them so that I shouldn't fall out.

I am well past the cradle stage.
I am three or four now!
I am living with my parents in a *dacha* at
the seaside near Riga,
what is now Majory and was then called
Mayorengof.
The branch of white lilac, in a glancing
shaft of sunlight, peeps in through the
window.

It sways over me.
My first conscious impression is — a
close-up.

Thus my consciousness awoke beneath a
lilac branch.

Then for many, many years just such a
branch as that would make it sink into a
half-sleep.

But the branch was not in fact alive; it
was painted, half drawn, half
embroidered in silk and gold thread.
It was on a three-leaved Japanese
screen.

For many, many years I would fall asleep
looking at this branch.

I don't remember when they began to
stand it round my bed-head.

But it seems it had always stood there.
The branch was luxuriant and curved.
On it there were little birds.

And a very long way behind it — through
it — were drawn the traditional details of
a Japanese landscape.

Little huts.
Rushes.
Little bridges crossing streams.
Sharp-nosed little boats drawn with two
strokes of the brush.

The branch was not just in close-up.
The branch was typically used by the
Japanese as a foreground through
which they drew the distance.

So before I became acquainted with
Hokusai, before my passion for Edgar
Degas, I was caught up in the charm of
foreground composition.

With it the tiniest detail in the foreground
is on such a scale that it dominates the
whole of the interior.

Then holes were somehow made in the
screen in two places by a chair.
I remember it with its two holes.
Then it disappeared.

I think these two branches brought two ideas together into one vivid impression: the idea of close-up and the idea of foreground composition as being linked organically and in stages the one with the other.

And when many years later I was seeking the historical forerunners of close-up in the cinema, I automatically began to look for them not in the portrait or still life but in the fascinating way in which a separate element of a picture starts to come forward out of the general organism of the picture and into the foreground. The way in which out of the general ground of a landscape — in which it is sometimes impossible to make out a falling Icarus or a Daphnis and Chloë — the figures begin to come to the surface, at first by their stature, and then gradually become so close that they break through the edge of the picture, as in El Greco's *Espolio*, and then a leap across three centuries — to the French Impressionists, who were strongly influenced by Japanese prints.

But as far as I am concerned the tradition of foreground composition was taken up by two Edgars.

Edgar Degas and Edgar Allan Poe.

The first was Edgar Allan Poe.

The vivid impression of the Japanese lilac branch probably determined the keenness of the impression made on me by the story of Poe looking out of his window and suddenly seeing a gigantic monster clambering over the top of a distant mountain range.

Then it becomes clear that it is not a monster of antediluvian proportions at all, but a humble mole-cricket crawling across the window-pane.[1]

The optical combination of this close-up foreground image and the mountain range in the distance creates the frightening effect so magnificently described by Edgar Allan Poe.

It is interesting to note that Poe's flight of the imagination could not be built on direct impression — the human eye cannot at one and the same time 'get in focus' such a powerfully prominent foreground and the clear-cut outline of the mountain range in the distance.

Only the camera lens can do this — and then only one lens, the 28 mm, which has the marvellous ability to distort the foreground, exaggerating its size and shape.

But I think that the white lilac branch and the plastic descriptive passage from Poe's horror story in some way probably determined my most effective and most sharply expressive foreground compositions.

The skulls and monks, the masks and roundabouts of *Death Day* in the Mexican picture. The white lilac branch becomes a white skull in the foreground, and the horror of the Poe story a group of monks in black cassocks in the background. And the whole amounts to the Catholic asceticism of the Jesuits, who are inflicting blood and

the stake on the sensual splendour of Mexico's tropical beauty.

The roundabouts of *Death Day* repeat the same tragic theme ironically.

Here the white skulls are thrown right into the foreground, to the point where one can almost touch them.

But the skulls are cardboard — masks of skulls.

And behind them, full size, whirl the roundabouts and big wheels of laughter, glimpsed fleetingly through the empty eye-sockets of the masks, and making them wink as if to say that death is nothing more than an empty cardboard box through which the vortex of life will always unwearyingly force its way no matter what.

Another good example is the combination in the same frame of the profile of the Maya girl and the whole pyramid of Chichen-Itza.

The incomparable compositions of the second Edgar — Edgar Degas — and the sometimes even sharper construction of Toulouse-Lautrec bring us back again to the realm of purely plastic creations.[2]

But the very interweaving of these descriptive and directly visual impressions had a quite special significance for me.

It was probably the link between painting and literature — both seen plastically — that I became aware of first.

'Foreground composition' is still one of my favourite forms of plastic expression.

In its most restrained form it is a simple taking account of the 'active' background — a taking account of what is going on in the interior while attention is being concentrated on the foreground.

In the period of the silent cinema it was done with great care and skill in America by Erich von Stroheim.

It must be said here that in his work this 'background' was limited not only in the social motivation of the situation of the action but also in the fact that his *fond* always played the role of a musical accompaniment realized in plastic terms.

So, for example, throughout one of the pictures Stroheim began with Mary Philbin (it was completed by Rupert Julian) details of a fair pass by, forming a background for the close-ups, and in the forefront is a roundabout.[3] And in accordance with their role as a kind of musical accompaniment to the main action the details of the fair — and in particular the roundabout — are out of focus.

The attraction of using these methods of composition is just as strong where the two planes — the background and the foreground — are thematically in opposition to one another as where the subject matter unites them. As is always the case with questions of composition, the methods are equally convincing in solving completely opposite problems.[4]

In the first case it is the maximum conceivable contrasting within a single frame not only of the planes of action

6

but also of volume (the roundedness of the foreground) and space (depth). And in such cases these methods of composition express the conflicting duality within a theme in the strongest way. (For example, a captain in the foreground looking into the distance — into the back of the frame — whence the enemy attack is expected.)

In the second case the same methods of construction are just as easily used in presenting the unity of the particular (detail in the foreground) and the general (the whole, occupying the background). (For example, a drum in the foreground beating out a march to which troops cross the frame like an avalanche.)

Of course, the way this kind of construction is read in different situations depends first of all on the thematic context, but also to a very great extent on the way in which other means of plastic expression are employed. (Here an important role will be played by the colour and light characteristics of the planes and by their tonal and linear treatment — their softness and harshness, their angularity and roundness, etc., etc.)

Of course, when the two cases come together in one composition this is particularly dramatically expressive — for instance, when the thematic unity of the contents of the foreground and the background is plastically resolved in the sharpest opposition — both in colour and in scale — between the background

(*fond*) and the foreground detail. In fact, one of the most impressive frames in *Ivan the Terrible*, Part One, was resolved in this way. It is the fairly memorable final montage of the scene in which the people come in a procession to Alexandrovskaya Sloboda to implore Ivan to return and rule again. There is an immense snow-covered plain with the thin black procession snaking out of the background. Against this — from the top and just outside the frame — hangs the enormous profile of Ivan, the top and back of his head sharply outlined and bowed in consent to return to Moscow. Here, with the harshest plastic contrast of scale and colour between the Tsar and the procession, what unites them is the inner content of the link that unites the Tsar and his people, the skilful detail of the head inclined in assent and the linear correspondence between the outline of the Tsar's profile and the contour of the movement of the procession.

My picture *The Old and the New* (1926–9) introduced into cinematography what became a particularly widespread fashion for this compositional device. The technique was developed and tried out particularly in this picture,* although

---

*This film also features the image of the 'bureaucratic machine' which, filling the screen almost to the point of overflowing, was represented as a grandiose, extraordinary and terrifying industrial contraption.

In fact, the carriage of an ordinary typewriter was used, photographically deformed by means of a 28 mm lens, but conforming with all the rules of composition in the foreground. (S. M. E.'s note)

Young Mexican boy

Daumier

I clearly recall my first attempts at this kind of composition as early as 1924 when I was working on *Strike*. These attempts of mine were not crowned with success because at the time my technical armoury did not include . . . a lens capable of such a shot!

Here I am mainly interested in the roads and crossroads by which I travelled and by which I approached the central problems which troubled me in different departments of my creative work.

The sweet venom of audio-visual montage came later. What concerned us in the silent cinema was montage and the role of the close-up, although it is interesting that even in the period of the silent cinema I was often seeking ways of conveying pure sound effects by means of plastic composition.

I recall how one October night in 1927, while I was shooting at the Winter Palace for the film *October*,[5] I was trying to produce plastically the effect created in a suite of rooms in the palace by the salvo of shots from the *Aurora*. The echo rolled through the halls and up to the room where the furniture had white covers on it and where the ministers of the Provisional Government were sitting wrapped in their fur coats waiting for the fateful moment — the establishment of Soviet power.

By using the system of opening and shutting 'iris' diaphragms in the right rhythm on to empty halls I tried to get this rhythm of the echo racing through the halls of the palace. What turned out to be more successful and to stick in the audience's memory better was the palace's crystal chandeliers, tinkling in response to the machine-gun shots in the square. Of course, more interesting from a methodological point of view was the attempt to get the graphic equivalent of the echo!

Things I read about and things that come into my head I visualize unusually clearly. This is probably a combination of a very great supply of visual impressions, a sharp visual memory and a good training in 'day dreaming'; you make visual images of what you are thinking about or remembering run before your eyes like a reel of film. Even when I am writing I am essentially almost 'outlining' with my hand, so to speak, the contours of what passes before me in an endless reel of visual images and events.

These impressions, which are above all sharply visual, cry out to be reproduced with an intensity which amounts to pain. Once I myself was the only means of such 'reproduction' — both as object and as subject. Now for this purpose I have a good three thousand 'man-units',[6] raised city bridges, naval squadrons, herds and fires to assist me.

But some thin coating of 'community' remains. Very often it is quite enough for me to reconstruct an alarming image that has been visualized broadly though not in every detail for me to be content with it and set my mind at rest. To a great extent, of course, this determines the special visual intensity of my *mise-en-scène* or close-up.

But often it serves as a barrier to other expressive elements which do not manage to fall into such an intensive creative line as that to which the visual side of my works submits.

The fact that my interest in some elements of composition and construction is disproportionately more intense than in others is obvious and beyond doubt. However, I prefer such a 'disequilibrium' to the classical strictness of balanced elements and I am prepared to pay for the charm of excess and sharpness in one area with flaws and inferiority in another.

But this does not all mean that the pre-eminence of the audio-visual in my works is a predilection for form over content, as some fool might think. The audio-visual image is the extreme limit of self-exposure outside the main motive theme and idea of the work. . . .

Text translated by Graham Webb and published for the first time in English Extracts from A History of the Close-up *(Autobiographical notes 1942–6) and from* Stereo-Cinema *(1947)*
Illustrations: drawings by S. M. Eisenstein

[1] It is a 'death-head' butterfly that appears in Poe's tale 'The Sphinx'. S.M.E. had forgotten the insect's name, but not the image.
[2] S. M. E. often mentions Toulouse-Lautrec's poster *Japanese Divan* as an example of this kind of composition.
[3] The film *Merry-go-round* (1922).
[4] One of S.M.E.'s basic theories: that the *same* solution can apply in two *diametrically opposed* situations; and that the same situation can be resolved in two diametrically opposed ways (the terrified woman stands up — or sits down abruptly).
[5] It should be remembered that the shooting of *October* (1927) interrupted the long work on the film *The Old and the New* (*The General Line*, 1926–9).
[6] To describe his 'human props' S.M.E. ironically employs the abstract bureaucratic formula in current usage throughout the 1930s.

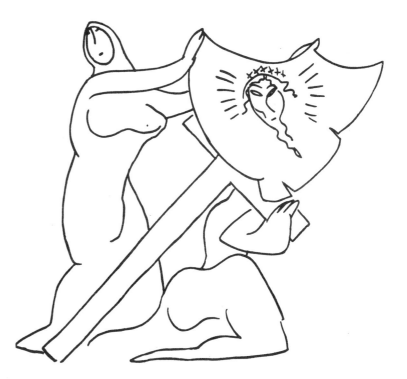

Mexican sketches: Ecstasy

BALLET

Dance

FILMOGRAPHY AND BIOGRAPHY OF EISENSTEIN

1898   Sergey Mikhailovitch Eisenstein born in Riga, 23 January. Father engineer-architect of Jewish origin, mother Slavic.

1905   Eisenstein's parents separate. Sergey lives first with an aunt, then with his father. He learns to speak fluent French, German and English.

1914–17   Architectural studies at the Petrograd School of Public Works.

1918   Enlistment in the Red Army where he works as a poster-artist in the psychological action division of Agit-Prop. Break with his father who joins the White Army.

1920   October. Demobilized at the end of the civil war, Eisenstein establishes himself in Moscow intending to study Japanese and acquire a knowledge of Kabuki. Meets up with his childhood friend Maxim Straukh and together they decide to devote themselves to the theatre.

1921–2   Designs sets and costumes for *Precipice, His Majesty Hunger* and *Macbeth* (the last in collaboration with Serge Youtkevitch); *Phèdre* for Foregger, *The House of Broken Hearts* for Meyerhold and *The Mexican* (an adaptation of Jack London) for Proletkult. He plans to create the Acrobatic Theatre.

1923   March. After producing a new version of *The Mexican* for Proletkult, he directs for them *A Wise Man*, a free adaptation of Ostrovsky with Alexandrov in the lead. He includes in this production a short satirical film, *Gloumov's Diary*, as an interlude.

In May he publishes in Mayakovsky's review *Lef* a manifesto on montage in the theatre and cinema. In the autumn produces *Listen to Moscow* by S. Tretyakov.

1924   Production of Tretyakov's *Gas Mask* in a Moscow chemical factory. New version of Fritz Lang's *Doctor Mabuse der Spieler* (1922), and *Gilded Rot* in collaboration with Esther Shoub. At the beginning of summer, still for Proletkult, he undertakes *Strike*, which is completed in December.

1925   28 March: premiere of *Strike*. Scenario and beginning of shooting of *1905* during the summer in Leningrad. Work on *Potemkin* from September in Odessa. The film is presented on 21 December.

1926   Journey to Berlin to present *Potemkin*. Begins work on *The General Line* then interrupts it to work on *October* for the occasion of the Revolution's tenth anniversary.

1927   Shooting and editing of *October*. For political reasons the showing of the film is delayed.

1928   14 March: public showing of the revised version of *October*. Eisenstein works all year on *The*

General Line. With Pudovkin and Alexandrov he puts his name to a manifesto on sound cinema entitled 'Orchestral counterpoint of image-vision and image-sound'. 7 November: premiere of *The General Line*.

1929 Travels outside Russia (with photographer Edouard Tissé and Gregory Alexandrov) to study sound cinema. Berlin, Lausanne, Paris, London, New York, Hollywood. In Switzerland he directs *Storm on the Sarraz*, a short burlesque, unfinished and now lost, for the occasion of the International Congress of the Independent Film.

1930 17 February: Sorbonne conference at which the showing of *The General Line* is forbidden by the Prefect Chiappe. Threat to expel Eisenstein. Numerous personalities from the world of arts and letters intervene on his behalf. Direction by Alexandrov of *Sentimental Romance*, to which Eisenstein agrees to put his name without really having participated.

May. Signs with Jesse Lasky a contract engaging Eisenstein, Tissé and Alexandrov with Paramount. Departure for the USA.

June. Joins Ivor Montagu in Hollywood. They plan several projects — *The Road to Buenos Aires*, *Bazil Zaharov* and *The War of the Worlds*. None of these are taken any further, but Eisenstein does work actively on the following scenarios: *The House of Glass*,

Black Majesty (in which Paul Robeson was to play the part of Toussaint Louverture), *Sutter's Gold* (after Blaise Cendrars) and finally a more ambitious project in which Eisenstein was extremely interested, *An American Tragedy* (after Theodore Dreiser). Like the others, the idea is turned down by Paramount (23 October).
24 November: signing of a contract with the American novelist Upton Sinclair. Sinclair and his associates agree to finance a film in Mexico. Eisenstein and his two collaborators leave Hollywood at the end of December.

1931 With Alexandrov and Tissé, Eisenstein directs *Que Viva Mexico*. Towards the end of the year relations with the producer deteriorate.

1932 15 January: Sinclair breaks with Eisenstein and orders him to stop shooting. The film is halted for good. Not being allowed to do any editing, Eisenstein returns to the USSR at the end of April.

1933 Without Eisenstein's authorization, Sinclair comes to an agreement with the producer Sol Lesser over the use of the negatives of *Que Viva Mexico*.

10 March: showing of *Thunder Over Mexico*, produced by Sol Lesser, edited by Don Hayes.

1934 November. Eisenstein takes up again the idea of a life of Toussaint Louverture and offers the part to Paul Robeson, then living in

Moscow. The project is not finished. Meanwhile, Eisenstein teaches aesthetics and production at the Moscow Institute of the Cinema.

1935 Eisenstein is bitterly criticized during the Assembly marking the fifteenth anniversary of the Soviet Cinema. He is taken to task by other directors who call upon him to undertake another film immediately or retire.

February. He chooses a scenario by Rzechevsky: *Bezhin Meadow*.

May. Beginning of shooting, interrupted in September by Eisenstein's illness.

1936 Intermittent shooting of *Bezhin Meadow* and troubles with the Russian Cinema authorities who demand a revision of the scenario. With Isaac Babel, he produces a new scenario. Shooting of the second version.

1937 17 March: Shoumiatsky, Director of the Soviet Cinema, violently attacks Eisenstein and interrupts production of his film.

25 April: Eisenstein publishes a public criticism of himself.

At the beginning of summer he starts work on the scenario of *Alexander Nevsky*. Shooting starts before the end of the year.

1938 Direction and editing of *Alexander Nevsky* which has its premiere on 1 December.

1939 February. Eisenstein is awarded the

Order of Lenin for his latest film. With the novelist Fadeyev he writes the scenario for *Perekop* (the project was abandoned). Preparations for *The Fergana Canal*, with a scenario by Eisenstein and Pavlenko. Departure for central Asia with Tissé. Shooting of documentary scenes. Production interrupted because of the war.

Appearance in New York of *Time in the Sun*, directed by Marie Seton from the negative of *Que Viva Mexico*.

1940 November. Production at the Bolshoi Theatre of Wagner's opera *The Valkyrie*, with sets and costumes by Eisenstein.

1941 October. With most of the other Soviet directors, Eisenstein leaves Moscow, threatened by the advance of Hitler's troops, for Alma-Ata, in central Asia, where a studio is being built. There he works on the scenario of *Ivan the Terrible*.

1942–3 Shooting of *Ivan the Terrible* at Alma-Ata and beginning of editing.

1944 October. Return to Moscow where he finishes editing the first part of *Ivan*.

1945 16 January: premiere of *Ivan the Terrible*, which is received enthusiastically. He finishes shooting the second part in Moscow (*The Boyars' Plot*), the last sequences being in colour.

1946 The Stalin Prize for the first part of *Ivan*.

February. Final editing of the second part. He falls ill and is nursed in the Kremlin.

4 September: the Party's Central Committee condemns the second part of *Ivan*.

20 October: Eisenstein again publishes a self-criticism.

1947 24 February: Interview with Stalin in the Kremlin together with Tcherkassov (Molotov and Zdanov are also present). Eisenstein suggests replacing the controversial scenes with sequences which were to have been included in the third part of the film *The Battles of Ivan*. He plans to shoot this entirely in colour.

1948 Eisenstein dies of a heart attack during the night of 9 February.

From Sadoul and Amengual

ESSENTIAL BIBLIOGRAPHY

Works by Eisenstein:

The Film Sense Faber and Faber, London, 1943
Film Form Dennis Dobson, London, 1951
Reflections of a Cinéaste in several foreign languages, Moscow
Drawings Albums, Moscow, 1961
Writings of S.M.E. in *Les Cahiers du Cinéma*, 1970–1

Works on Eisenstein:

Jean Mitry *S.M.Eisenstein* Paris, Ed. Universitaires, 1955
Marie Seton *Eisenstein* Ed. du Seuil, 1957
Léon Moussinac *Eisenstein* Ed. Seghers, 1964
B.Amengual *Eisenstein* Premier Plan, 1962

In the Avant-Scène du Cinéma collection, scenarios of *The Battleship Potemkin, October, Ivan the Terrible*

Anthology: *Eisenstein* by Rostilav Yourenev

Luda and Jean Schnitzer and Marcel Martin *Le cinéma soviétique par ceux qui l'ont fait* Ed. Français Réunis, Paris, 1966

Jay Leyda *Kino, a History of the Russian and Soviet Film* Allen and Unwin, London, 1960

Gloumov's Diary

1923

Credits

Idea and direction: Eisenstein
Photography: Evgeny Frantzisson

Cast
Ivan Iazykanov: Gloumov
Maxim Straukh: Milioukov-Mamayev
Alexander Antonov: Joffre
Ivan Pyryev: the Fascist
Vera Mouzykant: Mashenka
Vera Ianoukova: Mamayeva

Production: Proletkult with the help of Goskino

This is a five-minute short used as a cinematographic interlude in Eisenstein's production of Alexander Ostrovsky's play *A Wise Man.*

'The theme of Ostrovsky's play is that all a wise man needs is a little bit of simplicity. An important element in the plot is the diary in which Gloumov notes all his adventures. … We handled the complex subject of the adventurer's psychological game, as he adapts himself to the different people he meets, in an unconventional way by means of conventional costume changes. In the film-diary, we went further. By a risky extension of the idea and the use of fading techniques, Gloumov transforms himself into whatever object is desired by each person.

Frantzisson was shooting with me. And as at Goskino people thought that I might be too mischievous, so they gave me as a teacher … Dziga Vertov!

After the first two or three sequences Vertov left us to our own devices.

In all we shot 120 metres in one day.'

My First Film by S.M.E.

'Under the cover of buffoonery here is a collection of motifs which "react" on each other and whose sense becomes strikingly evident through those reactions. The idea was not in the facts nor in the dramatic expression of their consequences, but in the relations between them. It was "montage" before the word came into use.

This was theatre augmented by all the resources of the circus, music hall and ballet, but a theatre that finally disappeared behind all the things it wanted to annex. The little film of Gloumov's diary told of his acts and thoughts over a period of a week and reacted, because of the circumstances of its showing, with the "actual" situation of the stage Gloumov. *Gloumov's Diary* was, moreover, a kind of parody of the news films then being made by Dziga Vertov, Tissé, Kopalin and Belakov.'

S.M.Eisenstein by Jean Mitry

Strike

1924

Credits

Scenario: Valery Pletniev, Eisenstein,
I. Kravtchunovsky, Gregory Alexandrov and
the Proletkult collective.
Direction: Eisenstein
Photography: Edouard Tissé, Vassily
Khvatov
Sets: Vassily Rakhals

Cast
Alexander Antonov: working member of
the strike committee
Gregory Alexandrov: an overseer
Mikhail Gomorov: a worker
Maxim Straukh: the policeman
I. Kliukvin: an activist
I. Ivanov: the chief of police
Boris Yourtzev: the king of the
underworld
Judith Glizer: a woman

Production: Goskino and Proletkult
Shooting: Summer 1924
Completed editing: 14 December
Length: 1969m.
Premiere: 28 March 1925

In the original project conceived by
Eisenstein and the writer Valery Pletniev,
Strike was the fifth episode of a seven-
part epic entitled *Towards Dictatorship* (of
the proletariat). This series of didactic films
was to show the different aspects and
methods of the revolutionary struggle
before 1917 — demonstrations, strikes,
clandestine publishing, prison escapes, etc.

Shot with the Proletkult collective, *Strike*
departs from its didactic intention and,
using simulated newsreel and new
editing techniques, the theory of which
Eisenstein had already written about,
becomes a dynamic experimental work.

It is a film about not individuals but types,
and its hero is the mass in collective action.
At this time Eisenstein broke with Lev
Kuleshov, who favoured a cinema of
fiction, with characters related in a plot;
and he also left behind Dziga Vertov,
declaring: 'I don't produce films to please
the eye but to make a point.'

The film had a mixed reception in the
Soviet Union, where it was accused of
deviationism. It won a prize at the Paris
Exhibition of Decorative Arts in 1925.
However, its first commercial showing in
France had to wait until 18 January 1967,
at the La Pagode cinema, in a sound
version (with extracts from Prokofiev's 5th
and 6th symphonies).

Strike

At the factory everything is quiet. But the workers struggling to earn a pittance meet together to plan some effective action.

The situation gets worse. Hard taskmasters, the management and overseers tighten their controls.

The action committee starts preparing for a strike.

1 Two police informers exchange information about possible trouble-makers.

Informers in the pay of police and bosses are everywhere in and around the factory.

2 In a back room a man nicknamed 'The Monkey' prepares to hunt down the activists.

3 Another informer known as 'The Owl' disguises himself as a' worker so that he can mingle with them unnoticed.

4 The action group holds a meeting near the factory.

The idea of collective action is adopted. Leaflets are distributed calling on the workers to strike. Encouraged by the management, *agents provocateurs* recruited from among criminals get to work. A micrometer is stolen. The worker who was using it is accused of theft. The under-manager insults and threatens him. Unable to exonerate himself or bear the injustice, he hangs himself.

5 Angry fellow-workers cluster round his dead body.

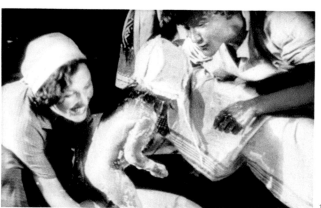

His death triggers off the strike. Brawls break out between overseers and workmen.

The men sound the factory hooters, the signal to down tools. 6

A general assembly of the workers votes for the strike. 7

Strikers break the windows of the administrative offices. 8

The under-manager and the overseer responsible for the worker's death are thrown into a muddy pond.

They emerge soaked and filthy. 9

Men cross their arms before their idle machines. 10

They are determined to stand up to anything.

A crow perches on one of the hooters. It will remain silent as the strikers spend the day at home. 11

Now at last they have some time to live and enjoy home life. 12

Meanwhile, harsh counter-measures are in preparation. Furious not to be able to fulfil orders, the manager decides to put an end to the strike.

The workers' assembly draws up a list of demands and sends it to the management.

13 While waiting for their answer, the workers hoot and jeer at the watchful police.

The manager and his associates decide to use all means in their power to put down political agitation.

14 At the end of their meeting, they drink to the success of their plan.

15 A servant picks up the strikers' list of demands, with which the capitalist has just wiped his shoes.

The strike continues. The workers run out of money. Famine threatens.

16 A starving child cries beside his empty plate.

His father's last tobacco has gone. The women sell their few objects of value, but it is not enough to feed the family.

17 Hugging her children to her, a mother bursts into tears.

In spite of severe pressure from the management, the strikers refuse to give in. The action committee organizes relief and distributes leaflets denouncing the cruel and hypocritical policies of capitalism.

Meanwhile, the informers carry on with their work.

The Owl secretly photographs an activist and sends the film to the chief of police. 18

At police headquarters, the young man is humiliated, beaten and tortured. 19

Submitted by turns to blackmail, threats and torture, he eventually cracks and betrays his comrades. The hunt is on.

Police in plain clothes recruit more *provocateurs* from among the local criminals. 20

They are given the job of setting fire to an alcohol depot near the spot where the workers are due to pass on one of their demonstrations.

One of them, a dwarf, slips into the warehouse and starts a fire. 21

But the workers are on the alert. They discover the plot and in spite of police efforts to hinder them, call the fire brigade. Unmasked, the police no longer bother to seek a pretext for their brutality.

The firemen are ordered to turn their hoses on the demonstrators. 22

One worker who tries to resist is overcome by the powerful jets.

He drowns in the mud.

A decision has been taken at the highest level to break the strike by force and bloodshed. Police surround the workers' living areas.

Their cruelty knows no limits.

Strike

23 A woman who rushes to save her child from the horses' hooves is whipped by the police.

24 A child is thrown from the top of a building.

25 The police chief orders the workers and their families to be hunted down and massacred.

26 The savagery of the forces of repression recalls the slaughter of animals.

The police fire into the crowd.

27 The ground is covered with hundreds of bodies.

Power remains with the law of the bosses. The strike has been broken. The workers have paid with their lives.

23

24

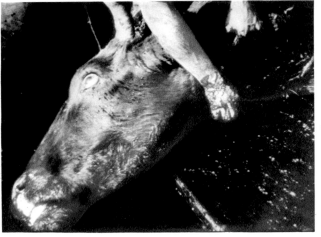

26

27

The Battleship Potemkin

1925

Credits

Scenario: Nina Agadjanova and
Eisenstein
Direction: Eisenstein
Chief assistant: Gregory Alexandrov
Assistants: Alexander Antonov, Mikhail
Gomorov, Maxim Straukh, A.Levchin
Photography: Edouard Tissé
Assistant cameraman: V. Popov
Sets: Vassily Rakhals

Cast
Alexander Antonov: Vakoulintchouk
Vladimir Barsky: Captain Golikov
Gregory Alexandrov: Lieutenant
Guiliarovsky
Mikhail Gomorov: Matoushenko
I.Bobrov: the conscript
Maroussov: an officer
Levchin: an officer
Repnikova: the old teacher

Actors and extras from the Proletkult
troupe. Soviet crews of the Black Sea
fleet and the people of Odessa.

Production: Goskino
Shooting: September – November 1925
Editing: November – December 1925
Length: 1740m.
Premiere: 21 December 1925, at the
Bolshoi Theatre

As for *Strike*, Eisenstein and the scenarist
Nina Agadjanova conceived the idea of a
vast fresco in eight episodes, *The Year
1905*, beginning with the end of the
Russo-Japanese war and Bloody Sunday
(when a peaceful crowd were fired on
before the Tsar's palace at St Petersburg on
9 January) and ending with the crushing
in December of the insurrection in Krasno-
presnia, a working-class district of
Moscow.

Shooting started in July at Leningrad but
was interrupted in August by bad weather.
But the Central Committee, who had
commissioned the film, wanted it for
December, so Eisenstein decided to
abandon the huge initial project and
concentrate on a single episode – the
mutiny of the crew of the battleship
Potemkin.

Potemkin marks a clear advance over
Strike, especially from the point of view of
construction – 'the organic unity of the
composition of the whole' – and of the
emotive impact of the editing, pathos
reaching the greatest tragic intensity in the
Odessa steps sequence.

In the reconstruction of events, Eisenstein
uses an idea borrowed from Goethe: 'the
opposite of the truth in the cause of
verisimilitude'. The detail of the production
often gives a historical force to what is
only the director's invention (the tarpaulin

covering the condemned sailors, the
massacre on the steps).

Presented at the Bolshoi Theatre,
Potemkin was an immediate success in the
Soviet Union and abroad (Germany, the
USA, Holland). It was shown in Paris by
the Ciné-Club de France on 12 November
1926, then. banned to public showing, had
only a non-commercial career until 1954.

At the Brussels Exhibition in 1958, *The
Battleship Potemkin* was voted 'the
best film of all time' by a jury of historians
and film critics.

The Battleship Potemkin

On 13 June 1905, the workers of Odessa begin a general strike.

1 In the harbour are several ships of the Tsar's Black Sea squadron, including the battleship *Potemkin*.

On board *Potemkin*, the revolutionary sailors Matoushenko and Vakoulint-chouk appeal for support for the Odessa strikers.

2 In their sleeping quarters, Vakoulint-chouk pleads for direct action:

'What are we waiting for? The whole of Russia is rising up. Shall we be the last?'

Next morning the angry crew gather around some carcases of putrefying meat.

3 The medical officer examines the meat.

Ignoring the men's banter, he folds his pince-nez and approaches the carcases.

4 They are crawling with maggots.

In a dry voice the doctor announces: 'These are not maggots, but flies' grubs. All you have to do is wash the meat in brine.'

The sailors protest but Captain Guiliarovsky, *Potemkin*'s second-in-command, brusquely dismisses them.

The rotting meat goes into the crew's soup.

5

7

On deck the crew prepare to go about their morning duties.

Later they refuse the contaminated soup and make do with a piece of black bread. Others buy food at the canteen.

The officers find an empty mess, the tin bowls lying untouched on the metal tables. 5

The ship's bugle sounds a general muster. The crew fall in on the after-deck. Captain Golikov addresses them: 'Those who found the soup satisfactory take two steps forward.' A few petty officers and two sailors step forward. The others remain motionless, even under the threat of hanging.

To break their obstinacy, the Captain calls for the guard of marines. 6

Matoushenko mutters an order: 'Everyone to the gun-turret!' At his signal most of the men move, but Guiliarovsky manages to cut off about twenty men. With the Captain's agreement, he intends to shoot them.

He orders the terrified sailors to be covered with a tarpaulin. 7

On the upper deck, the *Potemkin*'s priest prays to the Almighty to lead the sailors back to the true way.

Guiliarovsky orders the rifles to be trained on the tarpaulin.

8 Under the tarpaulin a few sailors fall to their knees. The marines raise their weapons.

9 Guiliarovsky's order 'Fire!' is immediately followed by a cry from Vakoulintchouk, 'Brothers! Who are you going to shoot?'

The riflemen hesitate, suddenly no longer listening to the officer's barked orders. Sensing the moment right, Vakoulintchouk gives the word of command: Come on, brothers, take up arms against these beasts!'

The hostages are freed from under the tarpaulin and the marines join the mutineers.

10 They surround their officers and attack.

The sailors plunder the armoury and hunt down the officers. Guiliarovsky escapes and goes after Vakoulintchouk. Brandishing his crucifix, the priest tries to bar the men's way. 'Fear the vengeance of God!' He is pushed aside and falls.

The crew throw their officers into the sea.

The medical officer leaves behind him a souvenir —

11 his pince-nez hanging from a rope.

12 The priest, who has been feigning death, opens a malicious eye.

But he is spotted and thrown into the sea like the others, forced to swim to the shore.

9

10

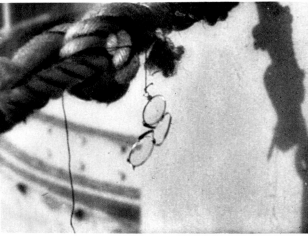

11

12

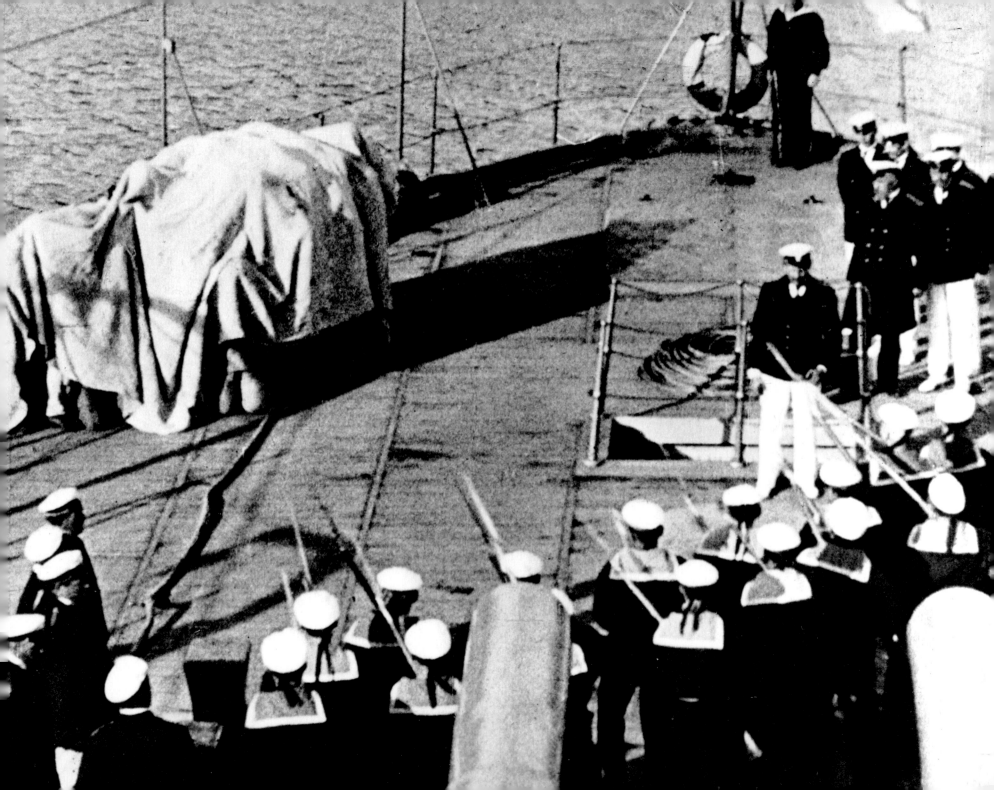

The Battleship Potemkin

The sailors are masters of the *Potemkin*. Meanwhile, in the forward part of the ship, the second-in-command shoots Vakoulintchouk in the back of the neck. Mortally wounded, he grabs hold of a rope.

13   His dead body hangs in the loop of the rope.

So, the leader of the mutiny is the first to die.

14   It is still dark. The port of Odessa sleeps, shrouded in mists.

The boat carrying Vakoulintchouk's body to the shore slips over the water.

15   Protected by a makeshift tent, the murdered sailor lies on the cobbles of the harbour.

A candle lights his face, and the words: 'For a spoonful of soup.' Passers-by stop. News of the *Potemkin*'s mutiny spreads.

16   Since dawn the people of Odessa have been coming down to the harbour to pay homage to the dead sailor and express solidarity with the battleship's crew.

17   'We must never forget him!' cries a woman in a black shawl.

She describes how he died and speaks of the struggle against Tsarism. The others support her, demanding vengeance.

14

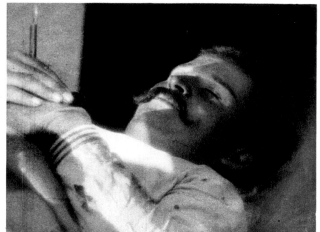
15

16

17

A bourgeois who sneers at the crowd's revolutionary ardour is violently taken to task.

Trembling with anger, a woman tears 18
off his scarf and cries out her hatred of
the murderers.

Like a river, the crowd flows down 19
from the streets and stairways to the
the harbour.

A feeling of power and solidarity
inspires them. 'The future belongs to
us!'

On board *Potemkin*, a meeting is held 20
between the mutineers and spokesmen
from Odessa.

The delegates inform them that the
Admiralty is preparing an attack. But
the crew's fighting spirit overcomes
their fear. The red flag is run up the
mast. A flotilla of small boats sails
towards the battleship as the people of
Odessa bring provisions for the men.

On the great steps leading to the 21
harbour, an enormous crowd acclaims
the victorious sailors.

Their faces are full of joy and hope.

An old teacher and a young schoolgirl 22
cheer the *Potemkin*'s red flag.

But suddenly, a rank of soldiers appears
at the top of the steps.

23 Their rifles, bayonets fixed, are pointed at the crowd.

Without warning, they open fire at point blank range. Leather-booted, moving down the steps with mechanical precision, they step over dead bodies. The people panic and scatter in confusion.

24 Under the statue of Richelieu they advance, spreading terror and death.

25 A few of the people seek refuge behind the blocks of stone bordering the stairway.

The others rush down the steps. A woman runs, holding her son by the hand.

26 The child is hit and falls.

27 The mother screams in fear and anguish.

All the way down these interminable steps,

28 men, women and children jostle and barge each other, desperately leaping over the bodies of the dead and wounded, their one idea to escape the raking fire.

Clutching her wounded child to her, the mother makes her way back up the steps.

29 A small group has tried to hide by the side of the steps. Crouching, terrified, they remain frozen to the spot.

The old teacher suggests they all stop running and beg the soldiers to stop the slaughter. In spite of their terror, they turn and plead with the soldiers to stop firing.

25

23

24

26

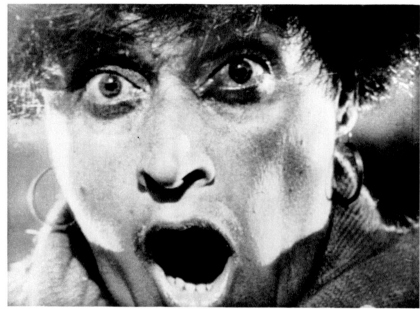

27

28

29

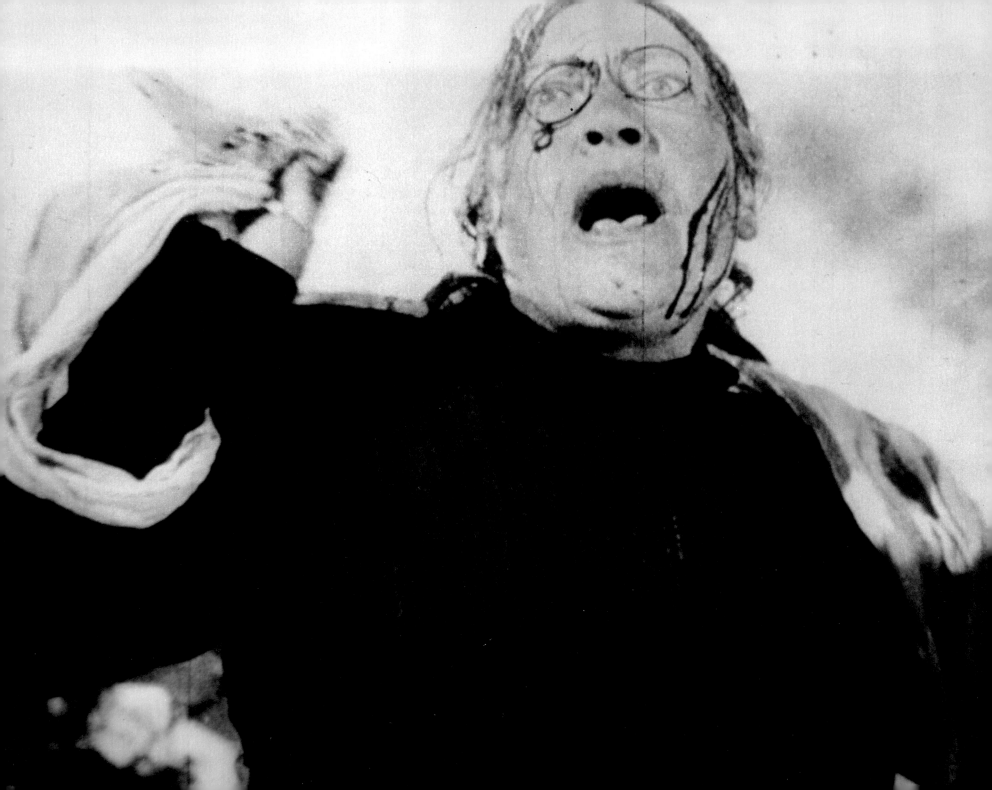

30

31

33

32

The mother carrying her bleeding child stops, facing the soldiers. 30

Her pleas are answered by bullets. Her dead body covers the corpse of her child.

At the bottom of the steps, the mounted Cossacks charge, cutting people down with their sabres. 31

Stranded, a young woman uses her body to protect the pram with her baby in it. The line of soldiers comes nearer.

The woman's beautiful face is contorted in a cry of terror. 32

Like some pitiless machine, the boots tramp down the steps. 33

Another volley. The woman, hit in the stomach, slowly crumples.

As she falls, she gives the pram a push. It gathers speed and bumps down over the steps, hurtling the baby towards certain death.

The old teacher, her face bleeding, lifts her arms in horror. 34

The fallen wounded beg the soldiers to spare their lives. A student sees the pram hurtling down, but his cry is useless.

On the steps and in the nearby streets, the massacre continues.

Slashing with his whip, a Cossack puts out one of the old teacher's eyes.

But then the guns of the *Potemkin* begin their reply to the Tsarist forces' savagery,

shattering the iron gate of the Odessa theatre.   35

The revolutionary forces rouse and counter-attack. We see in succession a stone lion sleeping,

and a lion raising its head,   36

and a lion rising and roaring.   37

36

37

The battleship's guns destroy the theatre, the palaces, the houses of the bourgeois. In the city and harbour, demonstrations continue until evening. A meeting is held on board *Potemkin* to decide a plan of action. The social-democrat sailor Feldman, a native of Odessa, appeals to the crew to put to shore, join the people of Odessa and destroy the Tsarist forces on land; but in the end they elect to confront the Admiralty ships preparing to attack them.

A long night of anguish and vigil is to follow. At dawn the alarm is given. The squadron is in sight. The revolutionary committee led by Matoushenko directs preparations for the battle. Every man has a particular task. At last the order to attack is given. Followed by the torpedo boat 276, which has joined the mutiny, *Potemkin* steams towards the squadron.

The Battleship Potemkin

38 Clustered on the bridge and on ladders, the sailors anxiously watch the enemy ships.

39 The great guns of *Potemkin* are trained on the flagship, ready to fire.

A sailor flashes messages to the other crews of the squadron: 'Join us!'

As the range gradually shortens, tension mounts.

40 Suddenly the strained faces relax.

First uncertain smiles grow into delighted laughter. The Admiralty's sailors have refused to fire on their brothers in *Potemkin*. Without a shot fired, she sails past the squadron.

41 The victorious mutineers cheer the sailors of the flagship.

38

39

41

October

1927

Credits

Scenario and direction: Eisenstein and Alexandrov
Assistants: Maxim Straukh, Mikhail Gomorov, Ilya Trauberg
Photography: Edouard Tissé
Assistant cameramen: Vladimir Nilsen, Vladimir Popov
Scts: Kovriguin

Cast
The worker Nikandrov: Lenin
Boris Livanov: Minister Terechtchenko
With the soldiers of the Red Army, sailors of the Red Fleet, workers and inhabitants of Leningrad.

Production: Sovkino
Beginning of shooting: 13 April 1927
Length: 2800m.
Premiere: 20 January 1928, at Leningrad

After the success of *Potemkin*, the Party's Central Committee asked Eisenstein to make a film on the October Revolution.

'Taking his inspiration from John Reed's *Ten Days That Shook the World*, Eisenstein and his co-scenarist Alexandrov first sought to include the whole history of the proletarian revolution – its preparation, beginnings, development and final victory. In the end the authors restricted themselves once again to a single episode: the events at Petrograd from February to October 1917.'

The film team had considerable means at its disposal, and *October* became the first Soviet 'epic'. Shooting took six months of intensive work and produced 49,000 metres of film. Thousands of extras were used in some scenes. The life of Leningrad was completely disrupted as its inhabitants found themselves transported back ten years.

A first cut of 3,800 metres was ready for the anniversary of the Revolution on 7 November 1927. But political changes in Russia – the expulsion of Trotsky from the Party and his forced exile – obliged Eisenstein to re-edit his film drastically.

At its public showing on 14 March 1928, all the scenes in which Trotsky appeared had been cut (the new version was of 2,800 metres).

Eisenstein declared: '*Potemkin* has something of the Greek temple. *October* is more baroque. Certain parts of it are purely experimental, using methods of intellectual creation which I believe will be developed. Personally, from the point of view of experiment, I find *October* more interesting.' (Reported by Alvarez del Vavo in *Rusia Alos Doce Años*, Madrid, 1928.)

Several sequences in *October* correspond to the theory of intellectual cinema developed by Eisenstein in 1926–7. To translate such abstract notions as Religion, Power etc, on to the screen he uses a symbolic technique. Seeking the principle of communicating 'messages' on film, Eisenstein wrote: 'The hieroglyphic language of the cinema is capable of expressing any concept, any idea of class, any political or tactical slogan, without recourse to the help of a rather suspect dramatic or psychological past.'

These ideas were bitterly criticized. The public failed to understand the director's intentions and the film never achieved the widespread success of *Potemkin*. For showing abroad, Edmund Meisel had composed a score. In the sound version shown in France in 1967, extracts from two of Shostakovitch's symphonies were used.

October

Moscow, February 1917. Demonstrators storm the Kremlin. An angry crowd attacks the symbol of autocracy — the huge statue of Alexander III.

1 **Peasants and workers climb the statue of the Tsar and throw ropes round it.**

The Tsar is trapped.

The February uprising means his imminent downfall. A great hope inspires the Russian people: land, peace and freedom for all.

But the promise is betrayed by a provisional government supported by the Church and the bourgeoisie.

At the front, Russian and German soldiers realize they are the victims of a meaningless war. The enemies to be overthrown are secure in their palaces. The soldiers leave their trenches and fraternize.

2 **An old Russian expresses his joy.**

3 **In token of friendship, Russian hats are exchanged for German helmets.**

But those in power have other plans. 'The provisional government will respect to the letter the obligations accepted with regard to our allies.'

4 **A government envoy hands over the message in a Petrograd embassy.**

It means a resumption of the fighting, more butchery.

5 An explosion interrupts the friendly meeting of the soldiers.

6 Surprised by the sudden re-opening of the front, a Russian seeks the safety of the trenches.

The Tsar has gone but, as before, the people suffer war and famine.

7 Exhausted housewives queue in front of an empty shop.

The beginning of April. Lenin returns to Petrograd and delivers an appeal that will become the Bolsheviks' watchword: 'Down with the provisional government! Power to the Soviets! Long live the Socialist revolution!'

At the allies' request, Kerensky, leader of the provisional government, launches an offensive at the front. It fails miserably.

In Petrograd the hot July days are full of mass demonstrations, meetings and parades. Some people want armed uprising, but the Bolsheviks, judging the moment not yet right, call for a huge peaceful demonstration. In spite of which the government opts for savage repression.

8 Shells explode among the crowd. The panic-stricken people scatter.

9 A white horse is hit and falls on the Neva Bridge.

The government orders the opening of the bridges to cut off the workers' districts from the centre.

10

13

14

Bodies litter the bridge. 10

Dead and wounded will soon all lie at the bottom of the Neva.

Like the white horse still dangling from 11 the rising metal platform, implacable.

After the massacre, repression intensifies. Soldiers continue to show solidarity with the workers, bearing in silence the insults of the bourgeoisie. The Bolshevik Party's headquarters are devastated.

Meanwhile, the leader of the government installs himself in the sumptuous palace of the Tsars.

Followed by his aides, Kerensky mounts the palace steps. 12

At the doors leading to the Tsar's apartments, the 'democrat' Kerensky shakes hands with the footmen.

He is eaten up with pride, like the 13 metal peacock spreading its feathers in swaggering display.

Arrogantly he enters the private library of Nicholas II where his first act is to sign the decree bringing back the death penalty.

Obsessed with power, he gazes at a statuette of Napoleon. 14

Meanwhile, General Kornilov at the head of a Tartar division is preparing to re-enter Petrograd in an attempt to

October

re-establish Tsarism, 'in the name of God and country'. Several military and religious symbols illustrate Kornilov's attack.

15 Among them, a Buddhist mask.

The workers of Petrograd decide to defend their city. Powerless and desperate, Kerensky throws himself on the Tsar's bed, seeking oblivion in sleep.

16 The statuette of Napoleon, symbol of his ambition, breaks.

The Bolsheviks organize themselves, free their imprisoned comrades and force the government to open the arsenal.

17 Directed by the Party, whose Central Committee now has its headquarters at Smolny, workers, housewives and soldiers distribute leaflets and arm themselves. They cut the railway line and manage to halt the advance of the Tartars.

But a confrontation with the formidable Tartars will be avoided thanks to the appeals of the Bolsheviks. Their leaflets speak a language understood by everybody: 'Bread! Peace! Land! Brotherhood!'

18 Russian and Tartar seal their friendship in a dance.

With Kornilov halted and Kerensky isolated, the Petrograd Soviet prepares for an armed uprising.

19 The Bolshevik Central Committee meets on 10 October with Lenin presiding.

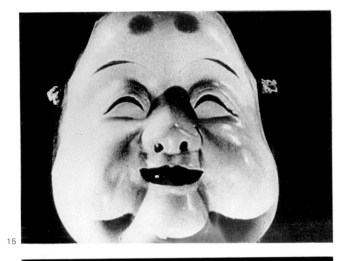
15

16

17

18

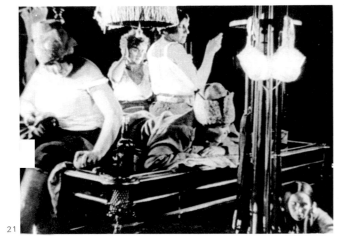

They decide to take over power on 25 October during the Congress of Soviets. **20**

The day comes. At dawn the cruiser *Aurora* approaches the city. Bolshevik sailors land and re-establish contact between the workers' districts and the centre, a contact the government has again tried to sever.

The distracted Kerensky appeals to the Cossacks for help, but they want to preserve their neutrality and desert him. He flees in a US embassy car. Officer cadets — the 'Junkers' — and women soldiers of the 'Battalion of Death' share the defence of the Winter Palace.

Before the battle, some of them relax on Nicholas II's billiard table. **21**

The anxious government drafts an appeal to the people. **22**

'The Constituent Assembly is the sole legal power on Russian soil.' Meanwhile, at Smolny, the Central Committee executive (Mensheviks and revolutionary socialists) open their Congress by affirming that the provisional government alone represents the popular power. In the city, the Bolsheviks control all strategic points. The Winter Palace is surrounded by Red Guards. An ultimatum is sent to the government.

Sailors mount guard on the Nicholas Bridge. **23**

24

25

26

The guns of the cruiser *Aurora* are trained on the palace. The women of the Battalion of Death, exhausted and demoralized, give themselves up one after the other.

At the Congress, a new bureau is elected with a Bolshevik majority. Agitators from Smolny get into the Winter Palace through the Hermitage cellars and persuade the Cossack artillerymen to desert their posts.

A Menshevik is derisively hooted by the delegates to the Congress when he declares that the army is not with the Bolsheviks. He has an immediate answer.

Banners expressing solidarity are raised on the platform by soldiers from the front. 24

Amid applause from the delegates, a man announces that the battalion of cyclists has come round to the Soviet cause.

Images of wheels and cycle gears alternate with those of clapping hands. 25

The Mensheviks are still not won over. 'We must smooth away these unfortunate differences without violence or bloodshed,' says one of them.

as if he were sounding musical harmonies. 26

Around the palace, the decisive battle has already begun. The signal for a general uprising is given.

And what of the Council of Ministers? 27 They are all puppets.

Salvos from the *Aurora* pound the palace. The Bolsheviks attack.

28 A crazed Junker pours bullets into the crowd.

29 Men fall, their blood mingling with the mud.

The doors are broken down and the people swarm inside. The last small group of Junker defenders is overrun and they flee.

30 A grim-faced officer fires point blank into the Bolsheviks.

The Bolsheviks pursue the defenders through the palace's innumerable rooms and into the cellars. The soldiers and sailors, sons of the people, are dazed by the luxurious apartments, the portraits of the Tsar's family, the bed canopy, the chests full of medals and decorations.

31 A sailor's hand rummages through the useless insignia.

'Why did we fight?' he asks.

The cadets are disarmed and searched.

32 The gold and silver cutlery hidden in their clothing is confiscated.

Sailors prevent the old women from looting the Tsar's wine cellar. Theft and revolution do not go together. In their anger, they break the bottles and stave in all the casks.

28

29

31

32

October

Antonov Ovseenko bursts into the Council Chamber followed by the people.

33 **He tells the ministers, 'You are all under arrest.'**

Then he reads the decree that marks the official assumption of power by the Soviets.

34 **'In the name of the military revolutionary committee, I declare the provisional government overthrown.'**

Clock faces mark the exact time of the Revolution in different parts of what will thenceforth be called the USSR.

35 **At the Congress of Soviets, Lenin speaks.**

He announces to the enthusiastic delegates: 'The working-class and peasant revolution has been accomplished.'

33

34

The General Line

1928

Original title: *The Old and the New*

Credits

Scenario and direction: Eisenstein and
Alexandrov
Assistants: Maxim Straukh, Mikhail
Gomorov, Alexander Antonov, A.
Gontcharov
Photography: Edouard Tissé
Assistant cameraman: Vladimir Popov
Sets: Kovriguin, Rakhals, A. Bourov

Cast
Marfa Lapkina: Marfa
M. Ivanin: her son
Vassia Bouzenkov: manager of the dairy
Kostia Vassiliev: the tractor driver
I. Youdin: the *komsomol*
Nejinkov: the teacher

Production: Sovkino
First shooting: 1926
Re-shooting: 1928
Length: 2469m.
Premiere: 7 November 1928

In 1926 Eisenstein, Alexandrov and Tissé
began work on *The General Line*, a film
that was to show in a quasi-documentary
and didactic way the workings of the
Party's new policies in Russia's rural areas.
The project was carefully researched. They
visited *kolkhozes* and *sovkhozes* and even
attended debates on agriculture at the
Party Congress.

Several sequences had already been shot
when Eisenstein, given the job of directing
October, had to interrupt work on the film.

Coming back to it in 1928, he realized that
circumstances had changed and that the
original scenario no longer corresponded
to the reality. A new one was prepared, less
theoretical, more closely inspired by village
life and its continuing problems. At the
centre of the film, he put a true popular
heroine, the peasant Marfa Lapkina. The
idea of 'types' so dear to the director of
Potemkin becomes much more flexible,
allowing a more subtle and sensitive style
of acting.

Without abandoning his theories of
'intellectual cinema' and its concomitant
symbolism, Eisenstein experiments here
with — and perfects — a more 'harmonic'
technique: 'Eisenstein uses not only the
"horizontal" impact of a succession of
images but the "vertical" impact of several
dramas, "lines" or different themes
simultaneously present in the heart of the
image. Through the organization of
dominant tonalities in certain sequences
(dark or light), or in the elements of the
image, Eisenstein reinforces the development of "lines" — intellectual (idea),
dramatic (suspense), and rhythmic (song)
— in a properly plastic action: a "toned"
drama.'

B. Amengual

The General Line

The October revolution that shook old Russia and made of her the first Socialist state did not succeed in changing overnight the ancient structures of the village. The power of the great landlords was effectively limited, but their wealth and influence was still considerable. The civil war, the still-powerful Church and ancestral customs all combined to keep the peasants in isolation and wretchedness.

1 **According to an ancient custom, when two brothers separated they divided all their possessions.**

So they were brought to the point of sawing a house in two, dividing a field, breaking up a cart. Every man for himself — and misery for everybody. In this village lives Marfa Lapkina. She owns a plough but no horse, a cow but no cowshed.

2 **The destitute peasants harness themselves to the plough.**

The results are cruelly disappointing. Desperate, Marfa asks the *kulak* to lend her one of his horses.

3 **She meets a flat and contemptuous refusal from the farmer and his wife.**

Harnessing her skinny cow, Marfa struggles to plough the dried-up field. The exhausted animal collapses.

4 **Marfa gives up, for fear of killing it.**

An agronomist sent by the administration arrives in the village and suggests to the peasants that they set

2

4

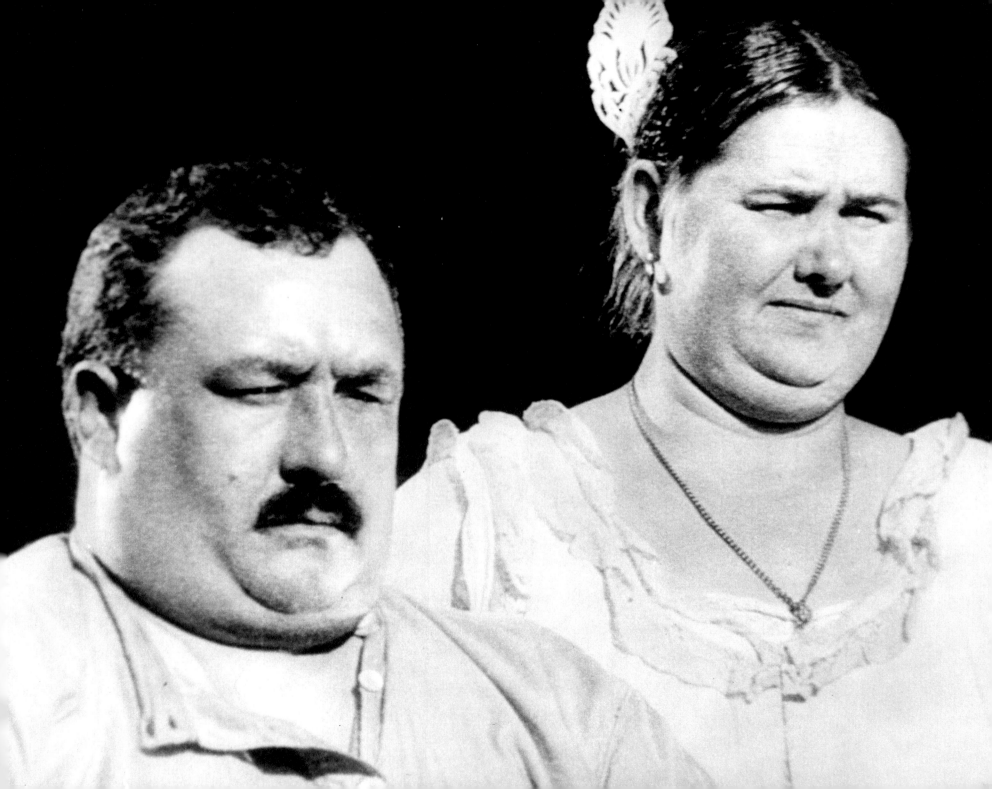

up a *kolkhoz*. The idea is not received with any enthusiasm and only four villagers — including Marfa — join the co-operative. The country is hit by drought. A long procession files behind the priest through the fields. The people carry candles and icons and chant litanies.

5 Following the priest, they prostrate themselves in the dust and pray for rain.

A cloud and a few drops of rain raise their hopes, but not for long. Their faith in the power of the Church is severely shaken.

The agronomist presents the co-operative with its first piece of equipment, a separator for making butter. The peasants watch fascinated as the gleaming new machine is started up.

6 Marfa's face lights up as she sees the first drops of skimmed milk.

The thickening butter marks a new era in the life of the village. Fifty more people join the co-operative. The profits from the butter-making are to go towards the cost of a bull.

7 But the treasurer shares the money out among the poorest peasants.

8 Marfa is furious to see the money squandered.

The men at first mock her, then threaten and bully her.

5

7

8

10

11

12

13

The agronomist arrives, saves her from their anger and recovers the money. Satisfied, Marfa goes to sleep.

She dreams of an enormous bull filling the sky and towering over a herd of cows.   9

'Rivers of milk flow from the clouds, a rain of milk falls from the sky . . . cowsheds, pigsties and chicken-houses rise up from the ground, all of matching whiteness. Houses sparkle in the sunlight.'

The dream becomes a reality. Marfa visits a model farm and buys a young bull.

Collective labour bears fruit:

The men work together gathering in an   10
abundant harvest.

The women gather ears of grain.   11

The village will not go without bread this year. The rational agriculture practised in the *kolkhoz* justifies the hopes of its pioneers. When Socialism becomes a reality in the whole country, poverty and misery will disappear.

Skyscrapers will replace the dirty   12
hovels, as in this futuristic vision of Kiev.

But there are still powerful forces against the new ideas, and saboteurs are active.

The *kulak*'s wife asks an old witch to   13
prepare a poison to kill the co-operative's animals.

The General Line

The other enemy is bureaucracy.

14   Remote and inefficient, government employees reign over empires of paper.

Accompanied by the agronomist, Marfa goes to see them and gives them a vigorous shaking-up. She manages to acquire a tractor, indispensable to the work of the co-operative. But the peasants are not at the end of their troubles: the bull of which they are so proud falls ill.

15   That evening they pray for its return to health.

And the recently acquired tractor has mechanical troubles. To repair it, the young mechanic makes use of anything he can lay his hands on.

16   Without any hesitation, he tears a strip off Marfa's skirt.

But even a smoothly running tractor is not enough to persuade all the villagers to give up their old ways and join the *kolkhoz*.

17   To show them the advantages of innovation, Marfa and the mechanic join all the carts of the village to their one tractor and drive past the astonished peasants.

At long last they are converted to the new system.

18   The final parade of tractors, sign of the mechanization of Soviet agriculture, confirms the success of the Party's 'general line'.

14

15

16

18

Que Viva Mexico

1931

Credits

Scenario and direction: Eisenstein
Assistant: Alexandrov
Photography: Edouard Tissé
Production: Mexican Picture Trust
(Upton and Mary Craig Sinclair)

After the failure of negotiations over the production of a film with an American background, Eisenstein expressed a desire to make a film in Mexico. On Chaplin's advice, he contacted the novelist Upton Sinclair, who agreed to collaborate. A contract was signed on 24 November 1930; its principal stipulations were that Eisenstein should have a completely free hand in the shooting, that the film was to be apolitical and that world rights as well as positive and negative copies should belong to Mary Sinclair. At Eisenstein's

request, the rights for the USSR were granted to the Soviet government.

Arriving in Mexico in December 1930, Eisenstein, Alexandrov and Tissé travelled the country from Mexico City to Yucatan. After several months, the project *Que Viva Mexico*, comprising a prologue, four episodes and an epilogue, was sent to Sinclair and the Mexican government. Both approved it.

The lack of finance, the magnitude of the project and the impossibility of developing film on the spot delayed shooting. Other difficulties accumulated. After eleven months in Mexico, the team had sent 37,000 metres of film to the USA. As they were preparing to shoot the last episode — *Soldatera*, the story of the women-soldiers of the revolutionary army and Emiliano Zapata's revolt in 1910 — Upton Sinclair, who two months previously had defended Eisenstein against Stalin's accusations of treason, suddenly interrupted shooting on financial, political and moral grounds. He refused to see Eisenstein and sequestered all the material already shot. In his autobiography, he was to explain that he broke with Eisenstein under pressure from his wife and her rich family. Demoralized by the failure of *Que Viva Mexico* and coldly received on his return to the USSR, Eisenstein was to wait four years before undertaking another film.

However, some of the material shot in

Mexico was used later in other films:

1933 *Thunder Over Mexico*, produced by Sol Lesser. Editing by Don Hayes. Material from the prologue, epilogue and the Maguey episode.

1934 *Death Day* and *Eisenstein in Mexico*. Two short films produced by Sol Lesser at the request of Upton Sinclair.

1939 *Time in the Sun*, directed by Marie Seton. Scenario and commentary by Marie Seton and Paul Burnford. Music: Mexican songs. Follows the basic scheme of the Eisenstein project. The pictures in this section are taken from it.

1941 *Mexican Symphony*. A series of five educational documentaries directed by W. Kruse.

1954 A provisional rough editing by Jay Leyda starting with 10,000 metres of film.

1958 *Eisenstein's Mexican Project*. A three-hour film of the rushes stored in New York's Museum of Modern Art (Jay Leyda).

Que Viva Mexico

Prologue

'The time of the prologue could be today, or twenty years ago, or 1000 years ago; because the people of Yucatan, a land of ruins and immense pyramids, have preserved the features and forms of their ancestors, the great ancient race of the Mayas.

Stones

Gods

Men

Act in the prologue.

In a time long gone …

.In the land of Yucatan, among pagan people, holy cities and majestic pyramids. The kingdom of death, where the past still rules the present — that is our point of departure.'

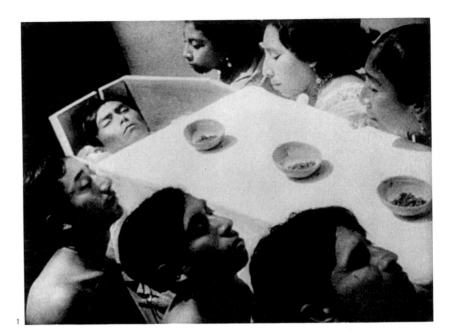

Like a symbol recalling the past, like a ritual farewell to the ancient Maya civilization,

1   a strange funeral ceremony is being enacted.

Death gives way to life. Dreamlike, the paradise of love opens

2   with the image of a young girl with bare breasts drifting along the river in a boat.

She combs her long, black hair and goes to see her lover,

3   offering herself to him with simple joy.

First Episode: the Fiesta

Before 1910 Christianity and the Indian religion met in the baroque style of the churches built on the sites of the ancient temples. The appearance of death and the universal reminder of suffering give a strange resonance to the Mexican version of the Passion.

4 Preceded by three skulls, a group of penitent 'monks' leads the procession.

An evocation of Golgotha.

5 On the way to the Cross, an old woman offers water to a thief.

6 The Christ and the two thieves are crucified on Calvary.

Second Episode: the Sandunga

'Tchuantepec, in the tropical forest, is the region where Spanish colonialism had least influence. The matriarchal system of the Tchuana Indians persists to our day.'

Concepción and Abundio marry.

Old women examine the bridal dress while friends bring the girl gifts. After the ceremony, the men perform a marriage dance in honour of San Diego la Sandunga.

7 Young girls watch the ceremony.

8

9

10

11

12

13

An old woman in search of her youth dresses in the same headwear. 8

The faces of the young couple are full of joy and tenderness. 9

Third Episode: Maguey

Llamos de Apam, on the high plateaux of the north, is famous for the production of a much-prized drink — pulque'. The peons who live in a state of servitude on the great haciendas extract pulque from a type of cactus known as the 'maguey'.

They work all day long under a burning sun. 10

The action takes place on the day of Corpus Christi, during the dictatorship of Porfirio Diaz at the beginning of the century.

During the ceremony, cock-fights mingle with Christian rites. 11

The originality of the ritual, which is a folk version of the Passion, lies in its masked dances.

The Christ and the two thieves. 12

A penitent submits himself to ceremonial chastisement. 13

As the ceremony reaches its climax, the young peon Sebastian goes to present his fiancée, Maria, to the owner of the hacienda. Custom demands that any peon wanting to marry must ask his master's permission. Maria is raped by a guest and kept prisoner. Guards beat up Sebastian and

throw him out. At nightfall he returns
with three other peons to free Maria.
A volley of shots greets them and they
run away. They hide in a maguey field.
One of them is killed, the others beaten
and tied up.

14   They stand waiting for their graves to
     be dug.

15   Buried in sand up to his chest,
     Sebastian is trampled to death by
     horses.

16   Crazed with grief, Maria discovers the
     mutilated body of her lover.

Epilogue: All Saints' Day

1931–2 – 'After the speeches of
Presidents and the orders of Generals,
death arrives dancing. Not one death,
but many. Many skulls, many skeletons.
What is it? The Carnival. The most
original, the most traditional of
costumed parades, *Calvera*, All Saints'
Day.' On this day Mexicans remember
the past and show their contempt for
death.

17   A girl laughs at the little skeletons in a
     display of toys.

18   The capitalist who wore the mask of
     joyful death reveals his true face.

'Life reaffirms itself under the cardboard
skulls; life surges forward, death
retreats and vanishes.'

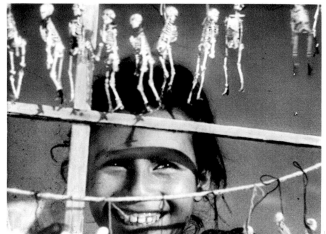

Bezhin Meadow

1935–1937

Credits

First version

Scenario: Alexander Rzechevsky, from one of Turgenev's stories in *Sketches of a Sportsman* and the true story of the murder of the pioneer Pavel Morozov

Direction: Eisenstein
Photography: Edouard Tissé
Assistants: Pera Dtacheva, M. Gomorov, F. Filipov
Editor: Elfir Tobak
Sound Technician: Leonid Obolensky
Music: Gavril Popov

Cast

Vitia Kartachov: Stepok
Boris Zakhava: his father
Elena Telecheva: president of the *kolkhoz*
Erast Garin: her husband
N. Maslov: the young arsonist
Nicolas Okhlopkov: a peasant

Production: Mosfilm
Shooting: May 1935 to April 1936

Second version

Scenario: Eisenstein and Isaac Babel
Dialogue: I. Babel
New actors:
N. Khmelev: Stepok's father
P. Arjanov: the political commissar
Shooting: August 1936 to March 1937

This being Eisenstein's first 'speaking' film, the matter of actors called for particular attention. The choice of Vitia Kartachov out of two thousand candidates to play Stepok surprised Eisenstein's collaborators. The part of the father was given to Boris Zakhava, an actor trained by Meyerhold and the Director of the Vakhantangov Theatre. Elena Telecheva, an actress of the Stanislavsky school from the Moscow Arts Theatre, took the part of the president of the *kolkhoz* and advised Eisenstein about other parts.

Shooting began in the spring of 1935. But in September Eisenstein fell ill and work was interrupted several times. Meanwhile, Boris Shoumiatsky, Director of Cinematography, had criticized the film's errors and asked for the scenario to be revised. In Eisenstein and Babel's new version there was less emphasis on the conflict between father and son, and the looting of the church by the *kolkhoz* workers was cut out. Certain other changes were made to give the film the correct gloss of Socialist realism. Nevertheless, Shoumiatsky used the pretext of high costs to order a complete halt to production and published a violent attack in *Pravda* (17 March 1937). Eisenstein had to criticize his own work publicly: 'I now see clearly the mistake, not only in the different parts but in the overall conception. The false conception was contained in the scenario but the director did not express any objection to it and continued to make the same mistakes, even in the second version.'

When and how did the material from *Bezhin Meadow* disappear? According to the official account, all the film stored in a certain Mosfilm strongroom was destroyed during a German bombardment in 1942. But it seems more likely that the positive copy was destroyed, on ministry orders, in 1937. The film's editor, Elfir Tobak, managed to save a number of frames which were used thirty years later in Naoum Kleiman and Serge Youtkevitch's montage of stills. We are familiar with it in the short, twenty-five-minute version. There is another — the 'scientific' copy of *Bezhin Meadow*, which is silent and lasts about an hour.

Bezhin Meadow

In an old village, Bezhin Meadow, the peasants have founded a collective farm. A few *kulak* landlords decide to oppose the idea. Unable to enjoy all their ancient privileges, they plan to avenge themselves by destroying the *kolkhoz*. Among the plotters is Stepok's father, a cruel, evil-tempered man who has just murdered his wife.

1   **Young Stepok and the peasant Blackbeard carry the mother's body away on a cart.**

'Why did your father beat her so much?' asks the old man. 'Because she understood me,' Stepok replies. Returning home, he finds his father in the company of other *kulaks*. All of them are drinking heavily. The father accuses the boy of spying on him and denouncing him to the authorities. He quotes from the Bible: 'If a son betray his own father, let him be slaughtered like a dog.'

2   **Threateningly, the father grabs the boy by the shoulders. 'I'll throw you in the oven and eat you!'**

The president of the *kolkhoz* arrives just in time to save Stepok and his little sister from the father's rage.

Under cover of darkness, the *kulaks* set fire to the tractor fuel depot.

3   **The peasants try to put the fire out.**

The fire-cart arrives.

3

3

4   Terrified by the flames, the horses
     panic.

     Ignoring the danger, Stepok climbs up
     on the roof of the depot and frees the
     pigeons locked in the dovecote.

     The arsonists hide in the church, which
     is surrounded. After a chase through
     the whole building to the very altar,

5   the peasants capture the saboteurs,
     including this young man.

6   An old woman confronts him outside
     the church.

     'Once we were a Christian people.
     What has become of us?'

     Armed peasants take the saboteurs to
     be tried in the town.

     In the fields, work continues with the
     harvest.

7   An old peasant sees the captured
     saboteurs approaching.

     The prisoners have to face the
     peasants' anger. Pitchforks and rakes
     are raised menacingly.

8   In the women's faces, contempt and
     hatred.

     'They wanted to bring back the Tsar!'

     Blackbeard steps forward, armed with
     an axe, having decided to take justice
     into his own hands. But Stepok
     intervenes: 'They are the last of their

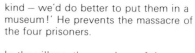

9

10

kind — we'd do better to put them in a museum!' He prevents the massacre of the four prisoners.

In the village, the members of the *kolkhoz* set up a special room in the church for meetings and festivals.

The old priest gazes at the figure of an archangel, already fallen and rejected.　　9

From now on, the faces of the peasant women will replace those of the madonnas.　　10

The transformation of the church takes on the atmosphere of a Dionysiac festival. An astonishing metamorphosis is born among this baroque splendour in the meeting of secular and sacred, in the contrast between old and new, Byzantine imagery and peasant earthiness.

The peasants who take Christ down from his cross unconsciously form the tableau of a strange and living Pietà.　　11

The night is mild. The children looking after the horses and the harvested grain sing round the fire.

But the arsonists have killed their guards and made their way back to the village, led by Stepok's father. Stepok notices suspicious shadows.

12 He sounds the alarm and gives chase.

A shot rings out. Stepok falls, mortally wounded by his father.

13 Ignoring the child's sufferings, the father repeats the terrible words of vengeance: 'If a son betray his own father, let him be slaughtered like a dog.'

The whole village joins in the hunt for the murderers.

14 A peasant carries the wounded boy to the village.

Stepok dies. All the village walks in his funeral procession. Young and old share the same grief and the same determination — to make of Bezhin Meadow a peaceful and thriving collective.

12

13

Alexander Nevsky

1938

Credits

Scenario: Eisenstein and Piotr Pavlenko
Direction: Eisenstein assisted by Dimitry Vassiliev
Assistants: Boris Ivanov, Nikolay Maslov
Photography: Edouard Tissé
Sets: Isaac Shpinel, Nikolay Soloviev, K. Eliseyev, working from Eisenstein's drawings
Music: Serge Prokofiev
Sound: V. Bogdankevitch

Cast

Nicolas Tcherkassov: Nevsky
Nicolas Okhlopkov: Vassily Bouslay
Alexander Abrikossov: Gavrilo Olexitch
Dimitry Orlov: Ignatius, master armourer
Vassily Novikov: Pavcha, governor of Pskov
Vera Ivacheva: Olga
Nikolay Arsky: Domache
Varvara Massalitinova: Amelfa Timofeyevna, Bouslay's mother
Vladimir Erchov: Grand Master of the Teuton Knights
Anna Danilova: Vassilissa, a woman of Pskov
Sergey Blinnikov: Tverdila, the traitor
Lev Fenin: the bishop
Naoum Rogojin: the black monk

Production: Mosfilm
Shooting: Spring to Summer 1938
Final editing: November
Length: 3044m.
Premiere: 23 November 1938, in Moscow

Faced with the growing danger of Nazi Germany and the need to mobilize the people in the defence of the USSR, the Party again called on Eisenstein and asked him to make a patriotic film.

To prevent any deviationist tendencies on the part of the director, he was surrounded by collaborators faithful to Party policy, notably Pavlenko for the scenario and Vassiliev for direction. Tcherkassov, who took the part of Nevsky, was a member of the Supreme Soviet of the USSR.

The historical epic *Alexander Nevsky* had to appeal to an enormous public, hence the simplicity of its plot, its folk character and general 'popular' treatment.

Developing a technique used in *Que Viva Mexico*, Eisenstein made sketches for the film before shooting because, he said, 'without some concrete notation of act and gesture it is impossible to be specific about individual behaviour. The drawing is very often the search for something. Sometimes the scene you shoot has apparently no longer anything in common with the drawing; sometimes it will be, even two years later, the drawing itself come to life.'

The famous Battle of the Ice was shot in midsummer, in the outskirts of Moscow, with artificial snow and ice. Here as elsewhere Eisenstein sacrifices the natural to the essential.

To the visual counterpoint present in the image itself (colour, shape, movement) and in the editing (rhythm, contrast), he adds here a whole spectrum of relationships between image and music. 'Thanks to the inspired collaboration of Prokofiev, Nevsky became the first masterpiece of a new art form — audio-visual art. The epic is built on the double development of the visual and musical movements. It is opera become cinematographic. It is the cine-plastic symphony prophesied by Elie Faure.'

Alexander Nevsky

Sketch for the battle of the lake

Studies for Alexander Nevsky

Some of Eisenstein's workin

Gavrilo and Bouslay

The blessing of the Teutons

Sketch for the first sequence of *Alexander Nevsky*

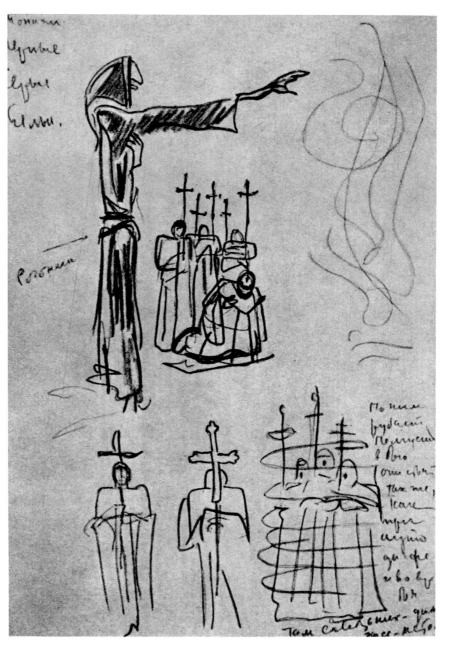

Alexander Nevsky

Russia is devastated during the first part of the thirteenth century by Mongol invaders from the East.

'Bones, skulls, burnt fields, charred buildings. Genghis Khan's Mongol and Tartar hordes reach the Caucasus, annihilate the flourishing Georgian civilization and advance into Russia, spreading terror and death.'

1 The Tartars ransack a village of peaceful fishermen.

At the risk of being massacred, the villagers refuse to pay tribute money.

2 Alexander Nevsky, prince of Novgorod, who lives among the fishermen, talks to the Mongol chief and manages to pacify him.

When the Mongol has gone, Nevsky delivers a warning to his people: 'A much more dangerous enemy threatens us from the West. First we must drive back the German.' The Teuton Knights are indeed extending their conquests eastwards and have invaded Russia.

3 In Novgorod market, Bouslay chooses a suitable axe at Ignatius the blacksmith's.

4 Two friends, Bouslay and Gavrilo, anxiously await Olga's answer. Which of them will she choose?

People converge on the great square from all parts of the city.

A messenger from Pskov announces 5
that this town has been captured by the Germans.

Traitors had been bribed to surrender it.

The merchants of Novgorod suggest buying back Pskov.

But other voices are raised — the voice of the people: 'We must call for Alexander.'

The knights Hubert and Dietlieb are 6
crowned princes of Pskov.

The new rulers, supported by cruel 7
bishops, spread terror in the conquered city.

Alexander Nevsky

8 Surrounded by faceless knights, the women of Pskov watch, horrified and powerless, the massacre of the innocents.

9 The German prince receives the blessing of the black monk as he throws a little child on the fire.

10 Those who dare to resist are bound and tortured.

11 From the gallows, the mayor utters a last cry: 'Go to Novgorod! Fetch Alexander!'

In a fisherman's hut, spokesmen from Novgorod ask Nevsky to undertake the defence of the country.

12 'We must arm the peasants and use them to conquer the Germans,' Nevsky replies.

9

10

11

12

13 The people take up arms at the prince's call.

Armourers and blacksmiths distribute all their weapons — pikes, sabres, axes. Olga promises the two friends to choose whoever is braver in battle. At the German camp, the knights attend Mass dressed in white.

14 The sinister black monk is the organist.

A messenger interrupts the office: the first of the Russians have just been sighted. The Germans prepare for battle. The opening skirmish gives them the advantage. Among the casualties is one of the finest Russian officers, Prince Domache.

15 Nevsky speaks a funeral oration and promises vengeance.

On the eve of the battle, round a bivouac fire, Ignatius tells the story of the weasel and the little rabbit. Seeing that he cannot outpace her, the rabbit runs between two birch trees planted very close together. The weasel follows and becomes trapped. He takes his revenge by deflowering her! The story inspires Nevsky's battle plan. The battle will take place on ice, which will be to the disadvantage of the heavy Teuton artillery. Bouslay, in the centre, must contain the German attack — the terrifying tactic known as 'the boar's head' — and hold out until Gavrilo and Alexander throw themselves on the enemy flank.

13

14

15

16

The Lake of Peipous (also called Tchoudsk), 5 April 1262.

Since dawn the Russian soldiers have been keeping watch on the frozen waste, waiting for the German attack. — 16

The Teuton Knights charge at full gallop. — 17

A fearful mêlée follows the first shock of impact. — 18

Defending magnificently, Bouslay and his men give ground and draw the enemy further into the trap.

Nevsky gives the signal to counter-attack. — 19

17

19

20 He throws his men on the German flanks. Russian cavalry attack from the rear.

21 Surprised, the Germans fall back.

22 Their units regroup in a square round the Grand Master and the Knights Princes.

23 A wall of shields and helmets known as the Macedonian phalanx is set up to break the Russian assaults.

Soldiers rush out from behind the wall for brief, damaging attacks on the Russian ranks and return inside the safety of the phalanx.

20

21

23

24

After several fruitless attacks, Gavrilo's men pierce the phalanx and it begins to collapse.

Always at the most dangerous spot, Gavrilo wards off the lances threatening Alexander's life.	24

To settle the issue, Nevsky takes on the Teuton leader in single combat.	25

The soldiers stop fighting to see the result of the duel.

The Grand Master is beaten and taken prisoner. Heartened by their leader's victory, the Russians attack on all sides. The Germans flee in disorder.

Their priests take refuge in their tents.	26

But the Teuton camp is destroyed and the priests executed. Vassilissa, daughter of the mayor tortured in Pskov, kills the black monk.

Ignatius captures the Russian traitor Tverdila, but Tverdila takes advantage of a moment's inattention to stab the blacksmith in the back.

'This coat of mail is too short', he	27
murmurs before he dies.

26

27

29

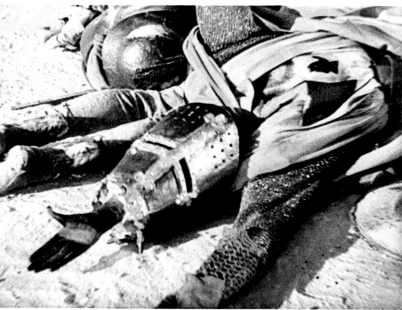

30

The rout of the Germans is complete. Officers and soldiers jostle each other in their scramble to reach the edge of the lake.

The bishop, who has escaped the Russian's vengeance, crawls over the snow among the dead. 28

Alexander's theory is correct: the thin April ice gives way beneath the weight of the Teutons.

Trapped in their heavy armour, the White Knights are swallowed up by the waters. 29

So ends the famous Battle of the Ice. It has borne witness to Nevsky's tactical genius and marked the Teuton Knights' worst defeat.

Night falls on the icy waste and the thousands of dead and wounded. 30

Broken lances and pierced helmets and useless swords litter the ground.

The scavengers are already at work.

31 A falcon takes possession of the dead body of a German.

By torchlight the Russians search for their wounded.

32 One of the victims is Bouslay. He is tending Gavrilo, who is even more badly hurt.

Olga finds them and they all return to Alexander's camp.

33 The liberated Pskov gives a clamorous welcome to Alexander and his army.

Prisoners and traitors are jeered by the crowd. After the victory parade, Alexander sits in judgment on his enemies. The Teuton leaders are exchanged for soap and their soldiers freed.

34 Harnessed like an ass, the traitor Tverdila is delivered to the judgment of the people.

31

32

33

For the young lovers, the moment of choice has come. Bouslay decides to marry the courageous Vassilissa. Olga will become Gavrilo's wife.

35 **The musicians blow their pipes and beat their drums.**

The people celebrate joyously. Alexander Nevsky delivers this warning to the enemies of Russia: 'He who comes with a sword will die by the sword.'

35

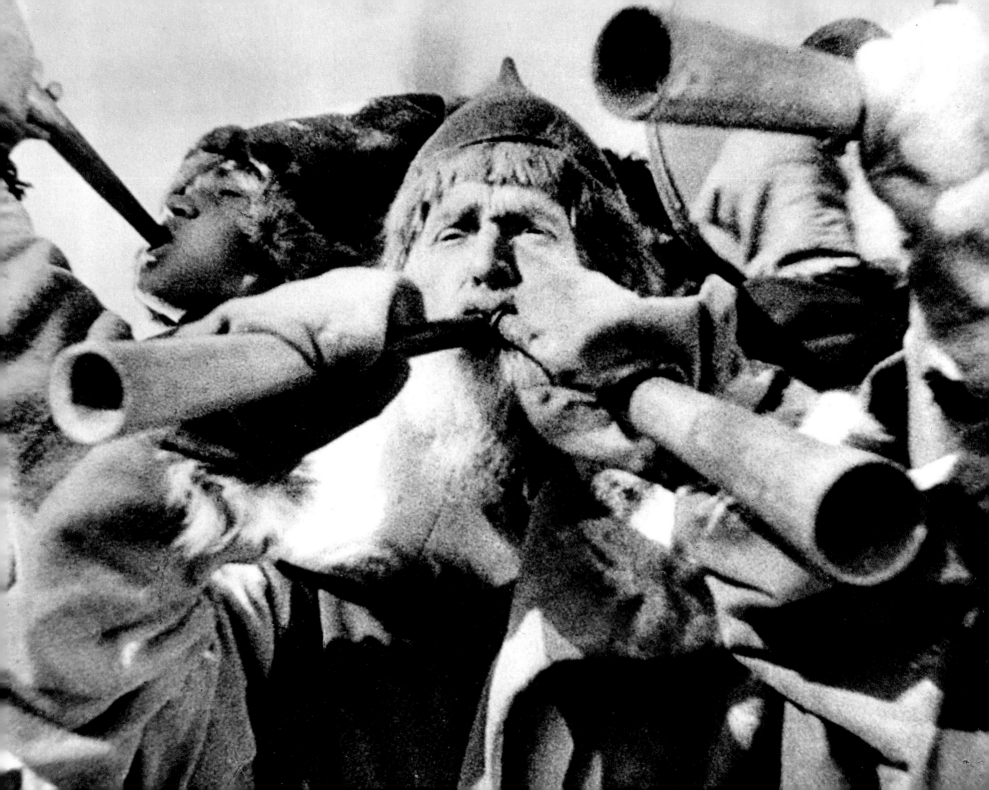

The Fergana Canal

1939

Credits

Scenario: Piotr Pavlenko and Eisenstein
Direction: Eisenstein
Photography: Edouard Tissé
Music: Serge Prokofiev

'The plan of the scenario was for an epic film dealing with the fertilization of the deserts from Tamburlaine's time to the building of the Fergana Canal in the modern soviet of Uzbekistan. "This will be", wrote Eisenstein, "the story of humanity's epic struggle against the deserts and sands of Asia and of the spectacular fight for water." It was in no way intended as a documentary.'

At the beginning of August 1939, Eisenstein divided the scenario he had written with Pavlenko into 657 shots. The main action — the fight for water and the fertilization of the desert with the help of the Fergana Canal — was preceded by a historical prologue showing the invasion of Tamburlaine, who, in the fourteenth century, diverted the water, so condemning the country to drought and death. This episode is introduced by a song from Tokhasin, the popular Uzbek singer, who evokes the drama and greatness of his country.

Eisenstein and Tissé made plans for shooting in central Asia. Shots of the construction of the canal were taken (the material was used elsewhere in a short documentary). But the size of the project, which was similar in scope to *Que Viva Mexico,* worried the authorities. The division of the scenario delayed shooting and necessitated revision of the script. With the escalation of the Second World War, production was cancelled.

Fergana: studies of racial types for extras.

Ivan the Terrible

1944–1945

Credits

Scenario and direction: Eisenstein
Photography: Edouard Tissé (exteriors)
and Andrey Moskvin (interiors)
Sets: Isaac Shpinel
Costumes: Leonid Naumova
Music: Prokofiev
Songs: V. Lougovsky
Sound: V. Bogdankevitch, B. Volsky
Cast
Nicolas Tcherkassov: Ivan
Ludmila Tzelikovskaya: the Tsarina
Anastasia
Seraphina Birman: Euphrosinia, the
Tsar's aunt
Pavel Kadotchnikov: Vladimir,
Euphrosinia's son
Mikhail Nazvanov: Andrey Kourbsky
Andrey Abrikossov: Kolytchev
Mikhail Jarov: Maliouta
Ambroise Boutchma: Alexey Basmanov
Mikhail Kouznetsov: Fedor, Alexey's son
Alexander Mgebrov: Pimene, Bishop
of Novgorod
Vladimir Balachov: Piotr Volynetz
Vsevolod Pudovkin: Nicholas, the fanatic

Part 1

Shot in the Alma-Ata studios (central
Asia) from spring 1943 to summer 1944
Length: 2743m.
Premiere: 16 January 1945

Part 2

Shot in Moscow from February to
December 1945
Length: 2373m.
Process: Black and white and Agfacolor
First public showing in 1958 after a long ban

photograph of the set

Additional material to Part 2

Erik Pyriev: the young Ivan
Pavel Massalsky: Sigismund, King of
Poland

Production: Mosfilm

In 1940 Eisenstein began work on a film
about the tsar who first unified all the
lands of Russia in the sixteenth century:
Ivan IV, known as 'the Terrible'. By April
1941, the main lines of the scenario were
sketched out. However, Eisenstein devoted
two more years to historical research,
analysis of Ivan's character and experiment
by means of drawings. The concept
matured and reached its final form in an
enormous three-part project: *Ivan Grozny,
The Boyars' Plot* and *The Battles of Ivan*.

'The first part, shot in the Alma-Ata
studios (in central Asia) from spring 1943
to summer 1944, came out at the
beginning of 1945. The film's success was
confirmed in January 1946 by a Stalin
award to the director and his principal
associates. By this time the second part
was also finished, having been shot in
Moscow from February to December 1945.
But on 4 September 1946, this second
part was condemned and banned by the
Party's Central Committee for "ignorance
of the presentation of historical fact".
Eisenstein was accused of representing
Ivan, "a man of great willpower and
forceful character, as feeble and insipid, a
kind of Hamlet" and "the progressivist
Opritchnik army as a band of degenerates".
This part had to wait for a public showing
until 1958.

At the time of his death Eisenstein was
working on the plan of the third part (its
title – probably provisional – was *The
Battles of Ivan*), which was to show the
vicissitudes of the consolidation of
Russian power and its outlet to the sea.'
Marcel Martin
'The film is not constructed as a story
whose action progresses step by step, but
as a poem. Each sequence is presented as
a "song" illustrating a particular moment
of the drama. ... Eisenstein seeks and
achieves epic sublimation through the
images themselves rather than through
their rhythmic and dynamic organization. ...
The movement is an intense one, and we
feel it profoundly when we see both parts
together. It is a gradual movement from
static to dynamic, a dynamism which was
really to come into its own in the third
part but which already explodes in the
banquet scene and colour sequences. In
these the composition takes its dramatic
and psychological significance from the
brilliant play of colours and their
astonishing mobility. Never had colour
been treated in this way – that is, less as
value than *sign*, or psychological symbol.'
Jean Mitry
In fact, Eisenstein was let down by the
poor technical quality of the colour. Was it
the Agfa film taken from the Germans at
the end of the war that was at fault, or the
Russian processing treatment (Sovcolor)?
In any case, the result was not up to
Eisenstein's expectations as he expressed
them in his writing (see especially 'Colour
and Meaning' in *Film Sense*).

The capture of Kazan

Ivan and Kourbsky

The death of Anastasia

Some of Eisenstein's working

The Procession

Remorse

Ivan the Terrible

Part 1 : Ivan Grozny

1   On 16 January 1547, in the Ouspensky cathedral, Ivan Vassilievitch, Grand Duke of Muscovy, is crowned Tsar of Moscow, absolute monarch of all the Russias.

2   Pimene, Archbishop of Novgorod, the officiating priest, blesses the congregation.

In muted voices, the foreign ambassadors express their anxieties and their hope that Ivan will not be able to impose his will.

3   The Boyars, gathered around Euphrosinia Staritskaya, murmur against the crowning of Ivan.

Euphrosinia, the Tsar's aunt, covets the throne for her son Vladimir Andreyevitch, a timid simpleton dominated by his mother.

After blessing Ivan, Pimene places the crown on his head.

4   He hands him the orb and sceptre.

5   Holding the attributes of power, the young Tsar turns to face his people. His look is stern and resolute.

6   The princes Kourbsky and Kolytchev approach Ivan carrying cups full of gold coins.

8

9

A shower of gold falls over the monarch's head and shoulders. Choir and congregation take up the chant: 'Long live the Tsar!' Ivan begins a speech addressed to the whole of Russia. He attacks the hated power of the Boyars and announces the creation of a standing army to be paid for by a tax levied on monastery and Boyar revenues. He proclaims his firm intention to win back the Russian territory in foreign hands.

These words fill the foreign ambassadors with fear and anger. They and Euphrosinia decide to take action during the marriage feast of Ivan and Anastasia.

On the table of honour, the married couple embrace. 7

As servants bring great goblets of wine, Euphrosinia slips out of the banqueting hall. 8

In the city, an alarm bell rings out: the Boyars have spread rumours of a catastrophe in the hope that the people will accuse the Tsarina.

Ivan questions his troubled friends. 9

Kourbsky avoids the issue but Kolytchev admits his disagreement with Ivan's policies and asks his permission to retire to a monastery.

photograph of the set

Ivan the Terrible

10 Servants appear bearing swan-shaped platters.

A crowd of people invade the ﹍lace courtyard, overrun the guard﹍ burst into the hall.

Their ringleader, the bl﹍ Maliouta, tries to strike﹍ heavy candlestick.

11 Kourbsky and Kolytche﹍﹍﹍r him ﹍d bear him to the floo﹍﹍﹍of the ﹍r.

A religious maniac denounces the family of the Tsarina Anastasia. He accuses them of witchcraft and of being at the heart of the troubles besetting Moscow. But Ivan deals with the situation like a true leader.

Messengers arrive from Kazan. The great Tartar city has repudiated its ﹍lliance with Moscow and declared ﹍ war. The great Khan has sent the Tsar a dagger, advising him to finish with life rather than suffer the humiliation of defeat.

12 ﹍n snatches the dagger from the messenger's hands and declares: 'We shall finish with Kazan once and for all!'

An enthusiastic cry goes up fr﹍ the crowd: 'To Kazan!'

11

12

13 The Russian army advances through the hills to Kazan.

14 Emerging from the imperial tent, Ivan and the Danish engineer Rasmussen examine the Tartars' imposing walls.

Under the direction of Maliouta, the Russians carry out Rasmussen's plan. They dig trenches under the walls and plant charges of explosives. Kourbsky ties up the Tartar prisoners in full view of the town to demoralize the the defenders. Rather than abandon their brothers to torture and humiliation, the archers of Kazan kill them.

15 Ivan reproves Kourbsky for his cruelty.

Maliouta detonates the casks of powder, blowing breaches in the walls.

16 Pushing cumbersome assault-towers, the Russians attack.

The cavalry under Kourbsky also attack; and the capture of Kazan confirms the Tsar's authority.

13

14

16

Ivan the Terrible

But on his return to Moscow Ivan falls
seriously ill.

17 A procession of bishops led by
Pimene performs the rite of extreme
unction.

18 Eyes staring, Ivan lies on his bed
clutching a candle.

Pimene places on the face of the
dying man the open book of the
Evangelists and murmurs:

19 'Lord, have mercy upon us.' A look of
terror crosses Ivan's face.

Euphrosinia meanwhile, in the course
of hatching a new plot, tries to win
Kourbsky over.

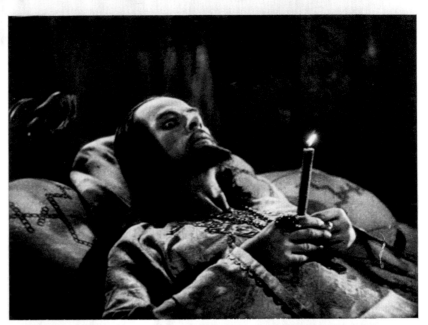

18

19

photograph of the s

20

23

She promises him absolute power if he vows allegiance to Vladimir.   20

Feeling the end near, Ivan asks everyone to vow allegiance to his legitimate heir, Dimitry. With closed faces, the Boyars turn away.

The Tsar falls to his knees and begs them to obey.   21

Before their hostile silence, Ivan gets to his feet and with his last strength curses their treachery. Believing the Tsar dead, Euphrosinia tries to abduct the young Dimitry, but he is saved by Anastasia. However, the aunt is not yet beaten. She demands the throne for Vladimir. Her faction take up the cry: 'Long live the Boyar Tsar!'

Kourbsky offers Anastasia love and protection. 'Together we could rule Russia.'   22

She rejects him and tells him the Tsar is still alive.

Opportunist that he is, Kourbsky vows allegiance to Dimitry, to the great surprise of Euphrosinia and Pimene.

Supported by Anastasia and Maliouta, Ivan makes his entry. He thanks Kourbsky for his loyalty and asks him to lead the Russian army against Livonia.

The prince kneels in obedience to the Tsar's wishes.   23

Ivan the Terrible

Ivan announces his intention to punish severely the Boyar plotters. Pimenc tries to intercede, but in vain. In the throne-room, the Tsar turns violently on the people who oppose his military campaigns. Fearing his fury, the Boyars flee.

24 Ivan orders his ambassador to carry a superb chess set to the Queen of England and suggest a trade treaty.

25 Ivan's immense shadow dominates the room.

26 The Tsar goes to see his sick wife and confesses his dejection. She is the only person he can confide in. He feels abandoned by his friends.

Hiding in the shadows, Euphrosinia spies on them.

The news from the front is bad. In the south, Alexey Basmanov cannot hold Riazan against the Tartar thrust because the Boyars have deserted him; in the north, Kourbsky's troops have been routed by the Livonians.

Still stricken with illness, Anastasia, who suspects Kourbsky of disloyalty, is steadily getting weaker. Ivan goes to fetch her some water. Euphrosinia quickly puts a poisoned cup by his hand. The Tsar gives it to his wife, who slowly drinks it.

24

26

photograph of the set

27 In the cathedral, Ivan grieves for his dead wife.

The news Maliouta brings is very bad: Kourbsky has turned traitor and fled to the Court of Sigismund of Poland, the Tsar's mortal enemy. The Boyars are stirring the people up to rebellion. Ivan jumps to his feet and violently denounces his enemies.

28 Carrying torches the people fill the cathedral.

On the advice of his bodyguards Maliouta and Basmanov, Ivan decides to surround himself with men of the people loyal to the crown, the Opritchniks. With them he retires to the Alexandrov Palace, declaring he will return to Moscow only at the unanimous appeal of the people.

Aged by his trials, Ivan waits. His hopes are not disappointed: from the snow-covered countryside rises a sound that grows louder and louder: 'Have mercy, Lord!'

29 An enormous human serpent winds its way over the white expanse towards the palace.

Ivan's wish is fulfilled. The people are calling for him: 'Return to us, our father!'

Ivan returns to Moscow 'to work for the future of the great state of Russia'.

27

28

photograph of the set

30

31

33

In Sigismund's ostentatious throne-room, the ambassador and Kourbsky, who are planning to carve up Russia, are seized with panic when they hear of Ivan's return to Moscow.   30

The Tsar makes a triumphant entry into the Kremlin and immediately delivers a warning to the Boyars. Kolytchev, who has retired to a monastery and taken the name of Philip, comes to see his old friend.

'Your enterprise comes not from God but from the Devil.'   31

Hurt by the sternness of one he still considers a friend, Ivan explains how the Boyars have been hostile to him since his childhood. At his father's death, they poisoned his mother. He himself has been ruthlessly exploited in their machinations. When he was a child …

Chouisky, the creature of the Livonians, and Belsky, the German agent, together watch over their young charge.   32

But in private they exert constant pressure on him to win concessions for their allies and accomplices.

Kneeling before the throne, the two traitors feign submission to the Grand Duke to ingratiate themselves.   33

When young Ivan proposes to take by force the towns conceded by the Boyars to foreign powers, the traitors mock him and insult the memory of his mother. Trembling with rage, Ivan has Chouisky arrested, so breaking for the first time the tradition of Boyar impunity.

He decides to reign alone, to be Tsar.

34   Finishing his story, Ivan confides in Philip his sadness, his loneliness, his need for friends. He proposes to make Philip Metropolitan of Moscow.

Taking advantage of this intimacy, Philip succeeds in imposing certain conditions.

35   The loyal Maliouta alerts Ivan to the priest's favouring of the Boyars.

He advises Ivan to act before the Boyars can do any more harm. Ivan agrees, then, seized with remorse, takes refuge in Anastasia's empty bedroom.

He is followed there by Fedor Basmanov, who reveals the cruel truth.

36   It was he, Ivan, who gave the Tsarina Euphrosinia's poisoned cup.

Ivan's terrible thirst for vengeance is not appeased by the summary execution of the Kolytchev Boyars. Seeing their bodies decapitated by Maliouta he says, drily: 'It is not enough.'

37   In his cell, the Metropolitan Philip grieves for his murdered brothers.

34

35

36

38

Pimene and Euphrosinia ask him to stand up to the Tsar and defend the Boyars. Sure of the power of the Church, he promises to win back the advantage during a service in the cathedral.

At his instigation, a mystery play is enacted intended to unmask the Tsar. The Chaldeans throw three innocent boys into a furnace on the orders of Nebuchadnezzar; but an angel comes down from the sky to save them.

The youths sing of the misery of a people ruled by a despot. 38

Ivan asks Philip's blessing. Philip refuses, denouncing his bloody acts and threatening him with the vengeance of heaven.

The hostility of the Staritsky Boyars confirms Ivan's suspicions about his aunt. He decides to be what they call him: terrible. Philip's arrest throws the Staritskys into a panic. To save all their lives, Euphrosinia decides to have the Tsar murdered.

Pimene selects Peter the Volinian for the task. 39

He also demands the sacrifice of 40
Philip, because 'a martyr is invincible, even for a Tsar'.

Terrified by the throne being prepared for him, Vladimir hides in his mother's arms.

She cradles him and sings to him. 41

39

41

Maliouta brings Euphrosinia a cup
presented to her by the Tsar
and to Vladimir an invitation to the
royal table. The boy obeys, arriving in
the company of Peter, the designated
regicide.

Discovering that the cup sent by her
nephew is empty, the old plotter
realizes that her joy was premature.

The Tsar's banquet is at its height.
The Opritchniks throw themselves into
a wild dance.

Ivan plies Vladimir with drink.
Basmanov is reprimanded by the Tsar
when he expresses astonishment at
this intimacy. The dance continues.
Maliouta discreetly points out to the
Tsar the suspicious presence of Peter.

42 Now completely drunk and over-
    whelmed by the Tsar's attentions,
    Vladimir reveals the plot against Ivan.

43 To avert the danger and make
    laughing-stocks of his enemies, Ivan
    enacts an outrageous comedy of the
    crowning of Vladimir, ironically
    prostrating himself before the
    simpleton.

    When the cathedral bells ring, Ivan's
    tone changes and he orders Vladimir,
    who is wearing the Tsar's clothes and
    regalia, to lead the procession.

44 Vladimir obeys.

43

44

Ivan the Terrible

45 In the shadows of the cathedral, Vladimir begins to understand the mortal danger he is in.

But it is too late. Peter stabs him in the back and he falls. Fedor and Maliouta seize the murderer. Euphrosinia runs up crying jubilantly: 'Ivan is dead!' She announces the succession of Vladimir.

46 But her joy is short-lived. Horrified, she sees Ivan approaching.

She realizes her terrible mistake and her reason begins to go. Clasping her son's body, she sings the cradle song with which she used to comfort him. Ivan releases the murderer, who has unwittingly left his hands free to deal with his foreign enemies.

47 Ivan the Tsar is now safe upon his throne.

45

46

154

We should like to thank all those who made this research possible,
notably the Cinémathèque Française, the Toulouse Cinémathèque,
the Grands Films Classiques, the Film-Makers Association of the
USSR, Galbafilms and the CDFC.